A WOMAN SPEAKS
Women Famous, Infamous, and Unknown

A WOMAN SPEAKS

Women Famous, Infamous, and Unknown

Lydia Cosentino

Dramaline Publications

Dramaline Publications
36-851 Palm View Road
Rancho Mirage, CA 92270
Phone 619/770-6076 Fax 619/770-4507

Library of Congress Cataloging-in-Publication Data

A Woman Speaks:women famous, infamous, and unknown/ [compiled by]
    Lydia Cosentino.
        p.   cm.
    Includes bibliographical references.
    ISBN 0-940669-30-7 (alk. paper): $12.95
        1. Literature—Women authors—Collections. 2. Women—Quotations.
    I. Cosentino, Lydia.
    PN6069.W65W62   1995
    808.82'45—dc20   94-49323

Cover art by John Sabel

This book is printed on 55# Glatfelter acid-free paper, a paper that meets the requirements of the American Standard of Permanence of paper for printed library material.

CONTENTS

(*continued overleaf*)

CONTENTS CONTINUED

INTRODUCTION

In fiction and in history, women have struggled to define who they are as individuals and as women. Questions abound: Are women equal to men? Subordinate to men? Superior to men? Do they occupy a separate sphere?

Do they belong in public or in the home? Is domestic work equal to, better than, or inferior to a trade or a profession? If a woman doesn't marry, what role does she have in society? Can she be educated? Should she be educated? To what end? Is love the center of a woman's life? Should it be? Is she a whore? Is she a saint?

During the last century, all of these questions and more occupied women. In diaries, letters, speeches, and accounts written by historical figures, and in words spoken by fictional heroines, we hear women giving their own answers, and those answers vary as the women who speak them vary. The voice of a slave recounts the tension and horror of escaping the nightmare of slavery; a mother describes sending her small children to work on work gangs; a young girl, after being seduced by a wealthy neighbor, describes the agony of giving birth alone and friendless and burying her unwanted baby, whose cries continue to haunt her mind; women speculate on what it means to be an "old maid"—some with joy, some with fear, some with acceptance; a middle-class woman who wants to work describes the stultifying duties of a daughter; an older sister describes how she "tricked" her younger sisters into wearing corsets; a journalist bewails the moral failure of "the girl of the period"; a female astronomer describes the difficulty of acquiring a needed education; a maid recounts the hardships of domestic duties; a judge's wife pleads for the recognition of sistership between prostitutes and respectable women; a vain girl muses on her beauty; the widow of a well-known author exhorts a young girl to think carefully before marrying; a female doctor refutes a male doctor's contention that women are constitutionally unfit to work; a Japanese woman describes her marriage at age twenty-nine and how she learned to love her husband after marriage; a young wife discovers a sense of freedom after her husband's death; a British visitor describes hearing a female speaker in nineteenth-century America; a woman explains why women are inherently opposed to war; feminists exhort men to give up trying to control women or their bodies.

These writings give voice and form to the many women in the past century who remind us how multi-textured their lives were and how many of them spoke up and spoke out for themselves or through the voices of their characters. They dispel any false ideas that women were silent in the past any more than they are silent today. and these voices sound uncomfortably familiar in the late twentieth century. Our foremothers spoke loudly from prairies, from cities, from factories, and from sitting-rooms—and their voices may once more be heard in the voices of their young ancestresses who seek a profession as a choice they inherited from these now-dead but still not silent women.

JANE EYRE

In this passage from Jane Eyre, *the heroine, an orphan, plain and without connections, has been forced to go out to work as a governess in an isolated house on the moors. Most of the time Jane is able to handle with seeming tranquillity the lot fate has condemned her to—she does not chafe at poverty or hard work or lack of family, but to be deprived of all opportunity of wider experience in the larger world just because she is a woman is, at times, unbearable. She does not repine for wealth or for finery or for love but for adventure, for experience, for life in all its rich wonder—denied her because she is not a man. When her restless discontent overwhelms her, she climbs up three flights of stairs, through the attic trap-door, to the leads, to look out beyond the limits of her circumscribed world and voice her unrest and her anger.*

Anybody may blame me who likes, when I add further, that, now and then, when I took a walk by myself in the grounds; when I went down to the gates and looked through them along the road; or when, while Adèle played with her nurse, and Mrs. Fairfax made jellies in the store-room, I climbed the three staircases, raised the trap-door of the attic, and having reached the leads, looked out afar over sequestered field and hill, and along dim sky-line—that then I longed for a power of vision which might overpass that limit; which might reach the busy world, towns, regions full of life I had heard of but never seen, that then I desired more of practical experience than I possessed; more of intercourse with my kind, of acquaintance with variety of character, than was here within my reach. I valued what was good in Mrs. Fairfax and what was good in Adèle, but I believed in the existence of other and more vivid kinds of goodness, and what I believed in I wished to behold.

Who blames me? Many, no doubt; and I shall be called discontented. I could not help it: the restlessness was in my nature; it agitated me to pain sometimes. Then my sole relief was to walk along the corridor of the third story, backwards and forwards, safe in the silence and solitude of the spot, and allow my mind's eye to dwell on whatever bright visions rose before it—and, certainly, they were many and glowing; to let my heart be heaved by the exultant movement, which, while it swelled it in trouble, expanded it with life; and, best of all, to open my inward ear to a tale that was never ended—a tale my imagination created and narrated continuously; quickened with all of incident, life, fire, feeling, that I desired and had not in my actual existence.

It is in vain to say human beings ought to be satisfied with tranquillity: they must have action; and they will make it if they cannot find it. Millions are condemned to a stiller doom than mine, and millions are in silent revolt against their lot. Nobody knows how many rebellions besides political rebellions ferment in the masses of life which people earth. Women are supposed to be very calm generally: but women feel just as men feel; they need exercise for their faculties, and a field for their efforts as much as their brothers do; they suffer from too rigid a constraint, too absolute a stagnation, precisely as men would suffer; and it is narrowed-minded in their more privileged fellow-creatures to say that they ought to confine themselves to making puddings and knitting stockings, to playing on the piano and embroidering bags. It is thoughtless to condemn them, or laugh at them, if they seek to do more or learn more than custom has pronounced necessary for their sex.

CAROLINE HELSTONE

Caroline Helstone in Charlotte Brontë's Shirley *thinks with dread of being an old maid after she discovers that the man she loves does not love her. The bleakness of the future she envisions haunted many young girls' minds of that period.*

I have to live, perhaps, till seventy years. As far as I know, I have good health: half a century of existence may lie before me. How am I to occupy it? What am I to do to fill the interval of time which spreads between me and the grave?

I shall not be married, it appears, I suppose, as Robert does not care for me; I shall never have a husband to love, nor little children to take care of. Till lately I had reckoned securely on the duties and affections of wife and mother to occupy my existence. I considered, somehow, as a matter of course, that I was growing up to the ordinary destiny, and never troubled myself to seek any other; but now, I perceive plainly, I may have been mistaken. Probably I shall be an old maid. I shall live to see Robert married to someone else, some rich lady: I shall never marry. What was I created for, I wonder? Where is my place in the world?

Ah! I see; that is the question which most old maids are puzzled to solve: other people solve it for them by saying, "Your place is to do good to others, to be helpful whenever help is wanted." That is right in some measure, and a very convenient doctrine for the people who hold it; but I perceive that certain sets of human beings are very apt to maintain that other sets should give up their lives to them and their service, and then they requite them by praise: they call them devoted and virtuous. Is this enough? Is it to live? Is there not a terrible hollowness, mockery, want, craving in that existence which is given away to others, for want of something of your own to bestow it on? I suspect there is. Does virtue lie in abnegation of self? I do not believe it. Undue humility makes tyranny; weak concession creates selfishness. The Romish religion especially teaches renunciation of self, submission to others, and nowhere are found so many grasping tyrants as in the ranks of the Romish priesthood. Each human being has his share of rights. I suspect it would conduce to the happiness and welfare of all if each knew his allotment and held to it as tenaciously as the martyr to his creed. Queer thoughts these, that surge in my mind: are they right thoughts? I am not certain.

Well, life is short at the best: seventy years, they say, pass like a vapour, like a dream when one awaketh; and every path trod by human feet terminates in one bourne—the grave: the little chink in the surface of this great globe the furrow where the mighty husbandman with the scythe deposits the seed he has shaken from the ripe stem; and there it falls, decays, and thence it springs again, when the world has rolled round a few times more. So much for the body: the soul meantime wings its long flight upward, folds its wings on the brink of the sea of fire and glass, and gazing down through the burning clearness, finds there mirrored the vision of the Christian's triple Godhead: the Sovereign Father; the Mediating Son; the Creator Spirit. Such words, at least, have been chosen to express what is inexpressible: to describe what baffles description. The soul's real hereafter, who shall guess?

GINEVRA FANSHAWE

In Charlotte Brontë's Villette, *Lucy Stone, on her way to take up a teaching position in Brussels, meets another young lady, Ginevra Fanshawe, traveling alone—a "girl, pretty and fair: her simple print dress, untrimmed straw bonnet and large shawl, gracefully worn, formed a costume plain to Quakerism: yet, for her, becoming enough." Unlike the serious, plain, and rebellious Lucy, this girl is quite practical and accepts her future cheerfully.*

Oh, the number of foreign schools I have been at in my life! And yet I am quite an ignoramus. I know nothing—nothing in the world—I assure you; except that I play and dance beautifully—and French and German of course I know, to speak; but I can't read or write them very well. Do you know they wanted me to translate a page of an easy German book into English the other day, and I couldn't do it? Papa was so mortified: he says it looks as if M. de Bassompierre— my Godpapa, who pays all my school bills—had thrown away all his money. And then, in matter of information—in history, geography, arithmetic, and so on, I am quite a baby; and I write English so badly—such spelling and grammar, they tell me. Into the bargain I have quite forgotten my religion: they call me a Protestant, you know, but really I am not sure whether I am one or not. I don't well know the difference between Romanism and Protestantism. However, I don't in the least care for that. I was a Lutheran once at Bonn—dear Bonn!—charming Bonn!—where there were so many handsome students. Every nice girl in our school had an admirer; they knew our hours for walking out, and almost always passed us on the promenade: *Schönes Mädchen*, we used to hear them say. I was excessively happy at Bonn!

Papa is called Captain Fanshawe: he is an officer on half-pay, but well descended, and some of our connections are great enough; but my uncle and Godpapa de Bassompierre, who lives in France, is the only one who helps us: he educates all us girls. I have five sisters and three brothers. By and by we are to marry—rather elderly gentlemen, I suppose, with cash: papa and mamma manage that. My sister Augusta is married now to a man much older-looking than papa. Augusta is very beautiful—not in my style—but dark; her husband, Mr. Davies, had the yellow fever in India, and he is still the color of a guinea; but then he is rich, and Augusta has her carriage and establishment, and we all think she has done perfectly well. Now, this is better than "earning a living" as you say.

MARY WOLLSTONESCRAFT

Mary Wollstonescraft is a radical feminist of the nineteenth century, but many of her ideas are radical even for the twentieth century. In the following speech, she argues that a woman should not concentrate all her energy on love.

To speak disrespectfully of love is, I know, high treason against sentiment and fine feelings; but I wish to speak the simple language of truth, and rather to address the head than the heart. To endeavor to reason love out of the world would be to out-Quixote Cervantes, and equally offend against common sense; but an endeavor to restrain this tumultuous passion, and to prove that it should not be allowed to dethrone superior powers, or to usurp the scepter which the understanding should ever coolly wield, appears less wild.

Youth is the season for love in both sexes; but in those days of thoughtless enjoyment, provision should be made for the more important years of life, when reflection takes place of sensation. But Rousseau, and most of the male writers who have followed his steps, have warmly indicated that the whole tendency of female education ought to be directed to one point—to render them pleasing.

Let me reason with the supporters of this opinion who have any knowledge of human nature. Do they imagine that marriage can eradicate the habitude of life? The woman who has only been taught to please will soon find that her charms are oblique sunbeams, and that they cannot have much effect on her husband's heart when they are seen every day, when the summer is passed and gone. Will she then have sufficient native energy to look into herself for comfort, and cultivate her dormant faculties, or is it not more rational to expect that she will try to please other men, and, in the emotions raised by the experience of new conquests, endeavor to forget the mortification her love or pride has received? When the husband ceases to be a lover, and the time will inevitably come, her desire of pleasing will then grow languid, or become a spring of bitterness; and love, perhaps, the most evanescent of all passions, gives place to jealousy or vanity.

I now speak of women who are restrained by principle or prejudice. Such women, though they would shrink from an intrigue with real abhorrence, yet, nevertheless, wish to be convinced by the homage of gallantry that they are cruelly neglected by their husbands; or, days and weeks are spent in dreaming of the happiness enjoyed by congenial souls, till their health is undermined and their spirits broken by discontent. How then can the great art of pleasing be such a necessary study? It is only useful to a mistress. The chaste wife and serious mother should only consider her power to please as the polish of her virtues, and the affection of her husband as one of the comforts that renders her task less difficult and her life happier. But, whether she be loved or neglected, her first wish should be to make herself respectable, and not to rely for all her happiness on a being subject to like infirmities with herself.

HARRIET MARTINEAU

Harriet Martineau (1802–1876), a prolific writer on public issues and pioneer in social science, wrote her autobiography in 1855 because she mistakenly believed she was going to die. Briefly engaged to a young man who went insane and died, Martineau never married. In this monologue, she claims she doesn't regret her decision to remain single.

I am, in truth, very thankful for not having married at all. I have never since been tempted, nor have suffered anything at all in relation to that matter which is held to be all-important to women—love and marriage. Nothing, I mean, beyond occasional annoyance, presently disposed of. Every literary woman, no doubt, has plenty of importunity of that sort to deal with, but freedom of mind and coolness of manner dispose of it very easily; and since the time I have been speaking of, my mind has been wholly free from all idea of love-affairs. My subsequent literary life in London was clear from all difficulty and embarrassment—no doubt because I was evidently too busy, and too full of interests of other kinds to feel any awkwardness—to say nothing of my being then thirty years of age; an age at which, if ever, a woman is certainly qualified to take care of herself. I can easily conceive how I might have been tempted—how some deep springs in my nature might have been touched then as earlier; but, as a matter of fact, they never were; and I consider the immunity a great blessing, under the liabilities of a moral condition such as mine was in the olden time.

If I had had a husband dependent on me for his happiness, the responsibility would have made me wretched. I had not faith enough in myself to endure avoidable responsibility. If my husband had *not* depended on me for his happiness, I should have been jealous. So also with children. The care would have so overpowered the joy—the love would have so exceeded the ordinary chances of life—the fear on my part would have so impaired the freedom on theirs, that I rejoice not to have been involved in a relation for which I was, or believed myself, unfit. The veneration in which I hold domestic life has always shown me that that life was not for those whose self-respect had been early broken down, or had never grown.

When I see what conjugal love is, the extremely rare cases in which it is seen in its perfection, I feel that there is a power of attachment in me that has never been touched. When I am among little children, it frightens me to think what my idolatry of my own children would have been. But, through it all, I have ever been thankful to be alone. My strong will, combined with anxiety of conscience, makes me fit only to live alone; and my taste and liking are for living alone. The older I have grown, the more serious and irremediable have seemed to me the evils and disadvantages of married life as it exists among us at this time: and I am provided with what it is the bane of single life in ordinary cases to want—substantial, laborious, and serious occupation. My business in life has been to think and learn and to speak out with absolute freedom what I have thought and learned. The freedom is itself a positive and never-failing enjoyment to me after the bondage of my early life. My work and I have been fitted to each other, as is proved by the success of my work and my own happiness in it. The simplicity and independence of this vocation first suited my infirm and ill-developed nature, and then sufficed for my needs, together with family ties and domestic duties, such as I have been blessed with, and as every woman's heart requires. Thus, I am not only entirely satisfied with my lot, but think it the very best for me—under my constitution and circumstances: and I long ago came to the conclusion that, without meddling with the case of wives and mothers, I am probably the happiest single woman in England.

ELIZA SOUTHGATE

Eliza Southgate (1783–1809), an eighteen-year-old schoolgirl, discusses a current theory of gender difference in this piece. Despite quoting Mary Wollstonescraft, a notorious feminist and liberal thinker, Eliza denies having feminist views.

As to the qualities of mind peculiar to each sex, I agree with you that sprightliness is in favor of females and profundity of males. Their education, their pursuit, would create such a quality even tho' nature had not implanted it. The business and pursuits of men require deep thinking, judgment, and moderation, while, on the other hand, females are under no necessity of digging deep, but merely "skim the surface," and we too commonly spare ourselves the exertion which deep researches require, unless they are absolutely necessary to our pursuits in life. Women who have not incentives to action suffer all the strong energetic qualities of the mind to sleep in obscurity. In this dormant state, they become enervated and impaired, and at last die for want of exercise. The little airy qualities which produce sprightliness are left to flutter about like feathers in the wind, the sport of every breeze.

Women have more fancy, more lively imaginations than men. That is easily accounted for: a person of correct judgment and accurate discernment will never have that flow of ideas which one of a different character might—every object has not the power to introduce into his mind such a variety of ideas, he rejects all but those closely connected with it. On the other hand, a person of small discernment will receive every idea that arises in the mind, making no distinction between those nearly related and those more distant, they are all equally welcome, and consequently such a mind abounds with fanciful, out-of-the-way ideas. Women have more imagination, more sprightliness, because they have less discernment.

The cultivation of the powers we possess, I have ever thought a privilege—or I may say duty—that belonged to the human species, and not man's exclusive prerogative.

I am aware of the censure that will ever await the female who attempts the vindication of her sex, yet I dare to brave that censure that I know to be undeserved. It does not follow (O what a pen!) that every female that vindicates the capacity of the sex is a disciple of Mary Wollstonescraft. Though I allow her to have said many things which I cannot but approve, yet the very foundation upon which she builds her work will be apt to prejudice us so against her that we will not allow her the merit she really deserves—yet, prejudice set aside, I confess I admire many of her sentiments.

CALAMITY JANE

Calamity Jane (Martha Jane Canary Dorsett Somers King Hickok Hunt Steers Dalton Wilson Washburn Coombs Buck Burke), the Heroine of The Plains, *Woman Scout, Wild West Heroine, is more legend than real woman, yet the real woman seeps through in the letters she writes to her daughter from whom she was separated since birth. Lying alone beside a fire in the western wilderness, she describes the hardships of frontier life without the usual romantic trappings.*

I sometimes find it impossible to carry the old album to write in, so you will find now and then extra pages. My ink has been frozen so many times it is almost spoiled. It is precious to me because your Daddy Jim sent it to me. You are getting to be such a big girl now, almost six years old. It only seems such a little while since I met your Daddy Jim and mother Helen O'Neil and gave you to them. Someday I am going to see you. I felt so bad when I heard of Helen's death. You are destined never to have a mother to live with. May God keep old Mammy Ross with you, darling. I am looking after a little boy. His name is Jackie, he is five years older than you, his father and mother were killed by the Indians. I found him the day your father was killed. He thought your father the greatest hero on Earth and saw him shot. He is a nice boy and will be a great man someday. The Sioux Indian are still troublesome. I went to the battlefield after Custer's battle and I never want to see such a sight again. In a house which had been dismantled was the carcass of a man apparently hidden there to escape the Indians seeking revenge. The squaws had cut legs and arms from the dead soldiers, then heads were chopped, then eyes probed out.

You see, Custer had molested an Indian village, running the squaws and children from their camps, so one can't blame them for getting even in their own way. Your Uncle Cy was in the battle, Janey. I found him hacked to pieces, his head in one place, legs and arms scattered about. I dug a grave and put his poor, poor old body in my saddle blanket and buried him. I can never think of him without crying. Good night, dear, till next time.

ABIGAIL ADAMS

In 1776, Abigail Adams, in a letter to Mercy Otis Warren, a play-wright, describes her attempt to convince her husband that women's rights are also of concern to the Revolution.

Mr. Adams is very saucy to me in return for a list of female grievances which I transmitted to him.

I thought it was very probable our wise statesmen would erect a new government and form a new code of laws, so I ventured to speak a word on behalf or our sex, who are rather hardly dealt with by the laws of England, which gives such unlimited power to the husband to use his wife ill.

I requested that our Legislators would consider our case and, as all men of delicacy and sentiment are adverse to exercising the power they possess, yet as there is a natural propensity in human nature to domination, I thought the most generous plan was to put it out of the power of the arbitrary and tyrannick to injure us with impunity by establishing some laws in our favor upon just and liberal principles.

I believe I even threatened fomenting a rebellion in case we were not considered and assured him we would not hold ourselves bound by any laws in which we had neither a voice nor representation.

In return, he tells me he cannot but laugh at my extraordinary code of laws, that he had heard their struggle had loosened the bonds of government, that children and apprentices were disobedient, that schools and colleges were grown turbulent, that Indians slighted their Guardians, and Negroes grew insolent to their Master. But my letter was the first intimation that another tribe more numerous and powerful than all the rest were grown discontented. This is rather too coarse a compliment, he adds, but that I am so saucy he won't blot it out.

So I have helped the sex abundantly, but I will tell him I have only been making trial of the disinterestedness of his virtue and when weighed in the balance have found it wanting.

I would be bad policy to grant us greater power, say they, since under all the disadvantages we labor, we have the ascendancy over their hearts "and charm by accepting, by submitting sway."

HARRIET JACOBS

In Incidents in the Life of a Slave Girl *(1861), Harriet Jacobs fought off the advances of her master, but she accepted the attentions of another white man, as she recounts here.*

Now I come to a period which I would gladly forget if I could. I will not try to screen myself behind the pleas of compulsion from a master, for it was not so. Neither can I plead ignorance. I knew what I did and I did it with deliberate calculation.

Dr. Flint's persecutions and his wife's jealousy had given rise to some gossip in the neighborhood. A white, unmarried gentleman knew my grandmother and often spoke to me in the street. He expressed a great deal of sympathy and wrote to me frequently. I was only fifteen years old. So much attention from a superior person was, of course, flattering. I also felt grateful for his sympathy. It seemed to me a great thing to have such a friend. By degrees, a more tender feeling crept into my heart. I knew the impassable gulf between us, but to be an object of interest to a man who is not married and not her master is agreeable to the pride and feelings of a slave. It seems less degrading to give one's self than to submit to compulsion.

When I found that my master had actually begun to build the lonely cottage, other feelings mixed with those I have described. I knew nothing would enrage Dr. Flint so much as to know that I favored another. I thought he would revenge himself by selling me, and I was sure Mr. Sands would buy me. With all these thoughts revolving in my mind, and seeing no other way of escaping the doom I so much dreaded, I made a headlong plunge.

At last Dr. Flint told me the cottage was completed and ordered me to go to it. I replied, "I will never go there. In a few months I shall be a mother." He looked at me in dumb amazement and left the house without a word. I thought I should be happy in my triumph.

But now that the truth was out, and my relatives would hear of it, I felt wretched.

I went to my grandmother. My lips moved to make confession, but the words stuck in my throat. I think she saw something unusual was the matter with me. The mother of slaves is very watchful. After they have entered their teens, she lives in daily expectation of troubles. Presently, in came my mistress, like a mad woman, and accused me concerning her husband. My grandmother believed what she said. She exclaimed, "Has it come to this? I had rather see you dead than to see you as you now are. Go away! and never come to my house again."

How I longed to throw myself at her feet and tell her all the truth! But she had ordered me to go and never to come there again. I walked to the house of a woman who had been a friend of my mother. When I told her why I was there, she spoke soothingly to me, but I could not be comforted. I thought I could bear my shame if I could only be reconciled to my grandmother.

My friend advised me to send for her. Days of agonizing suspense passed before she came. I knelt before her and told her things that had poisoned my life. She listened in silence. I told her I would bear anything if I had hopes of obtaining her forgiveness. She did not say, "I forgive you," but she looked at me lovingly with her eyes full of tears and murmured, "Poor child! Poor child!"

FLORENCE NIGHTINGALE

*Florence Nightingale (1820–1910) was from an upper-class family;
since she was considered the family beauty, her family expected her
to marry well. From an early age, however, she wanted to help those
less fortunate than herself. It wasn't until she was thirty that she was
finally released from family duties and able to begin her career as
the founder of the nursing profession. This excerpt from* Cassandra
*(1852) reflects on the spiritual and intellectual costs of a woman's
domestic confinement.*

Look at the poor lives we lead. It is a wonder that we are so good as
we are, not that we are so bad. Mrs. A. has the imagination, the
poetry of a Murillo, and has sufficient power of execution to show
that she might have had a great deal more. Why is she not a Murillo?
From a material difficulty, not a mental one. If she has a knife and
fork in her hands for three hours of the day, she cannot have a pencil
or brush. Dinner is the great sacred ceremony of this day, the great
sacrament. To be absent from dinner is equivalent to being ill.
Nothing else will excuse us from it. Bodily incapacity is the only
apology valid. If she has a pen and ink in her hands during the other
three hours, writing answers for the penny post, again, she cannot
have her pencil, and so *ad infinitum* through life.

Women are never supposed to have any occupation of sufficient
importance *not* to be interrupted, except "suckling their fools"; and
women themselves have accepted this, have written books to support
it, and have trained themselves so as to consider whatever they do as
not of such value to the world or to others, but that they can throw it
up at the first "claim of social life." They have accustomed themselves to consider intellectual occupation as a merely selfish amuse-
ment, which it is their "duty" to give up for every trifler more selfish
than themselves.

Women never have a half-hour in all their lives (excepting before and after anybody is up in the house) that they can call their own, without fear of offending or hurting someone. Why do people sit up so late, or, more rarely, get up so early? Not because the day is not long enough, but because they have "no time in the day to themselves."

If we do attempt to do anything in company, what is the system of literary exercise which we pursue? Everybody reads aloud out of their own book or newspaper—or, every five minutes, something is said. And what is it to be "read aloud to"? The most miserable exercise of the human intellect. Or rather, is it any exercise at all? It is like lying on one's back with one's hands tied and having liquid poured down one's throat. Worse than that, because suffocation would immediately ensue and put a stop to this operation. But no suffocation would stop the other.

The family? It is too narrow a field for the development of an immortal spirit, be that spirit male or female.

The family uses people, *not* for what they are, not for what they are intended to be, but for what it wants them for—its own uses. It thinks of them not as what God has made them, but as the something which it has arranged that they shall be. If it wants someone to sit in the drawing-room, *that* someone is supplied by the family, though that member may be destined for science, or for education, or for active superintendence by God, i.e., by the gifts within.

This system dooms some minds to insurable infancy, others to silent misery.

A READER'S ADVICE

Fashion has always been a bane to women. In 1870 girls were expected to rein in their freedom and become "ladies" by wearing corsets that were made with whalebone busk—a stiff slat about an inch in width that ran down the center to keep it flat. Many women claimed that tight-lacing was physically bracing and morally uplifting, but doctors warned of crushed ribs, stomach ulcers, headaches, dizziness and birth defects resulting from too-tight lacing. Young girls, previously accustomed to a certain physical freedom, did not always enthusiastically begin lacing as this account from the reader's advice column of the Englishwoman's Domestic Magazine, *June 1870, reflects.*

When my sisters were, the one sixteen, the other nearly two years younger, our mother considered it time that their figures, hitherto unrestrained, should be subjected to some control, and accordingly she laced them, rather tightly, in stiff new stays, both day and night.

They tried the usual expedients of cutting laces, and so forth, at first, but were entirely frustrated by mamma procuring a steel belt, fitted with a lock and key, to be worn at night outside the corset. I had then just left school, and the poor girls came to me in great trouble to know what they were to do. They confessed themselves doubly beaten; for the pressure of the stays, being an equal pressure, they were obliged to allow was not altogether unpleasant (although they could not racket about quite so easily); but the pressure of the belt, being unequal, was very uncomfortable indeed. Mamma was inexorable.

I proposed a compromise. The girls should be relieved from the belts and presented with very tiny-waisted riding habits (they were mad to be allowed to ride), which they should have facilities for using as soon as they could fit them on. They, on their part, should promise that their corset should be always tightly laced. The compromise was agreed to, but, although they tried their hardest—at first somewhat under protest—it was six months before the habits could be worn.

When I supervised their first mount, I can assure you I was very proud of my sisters' figures; and—dare I say—with the charming inconsistency of their sex, I believe they were, and still are, as proud of them themselves.

When the subject is mentioned, they will laughingly quote, *"Qu'il faut souffrir pour être belle"* ["One must suffer to be beautiful"], but they declare that the very slight suffering at first is fully compensated by the delicious sensation of perfect compression when once accustomed to it, and that they would go through it all again for that end alone if appearance were no consideration at all.

ANNIE BESANT

Annie Besant (1847–1933) tried to fulfill her own religious needs by marrying a clergyman, but she lost her faith and then her husband. She made a career for herself as a public orator, pamphleteer, and activist, but she lost custody of her daughter when her husband claimed she was unfit because of her advocacy of birth control and her atheism. In the autumn following her first lecture, she left her husband. She was a striking public figure with short red hair, a short skirt, and a loose blouse with a bright-red tie.

In that spring of 1873, I delivered my first lecture. It was delivered to no one, queer as that may sound to my readers. And indeed, it was queer altogether. I was learning to play the organ and was in the habit of practicing in the church by myself, without a blower. One day, being securely locked in, I thought I would like to try how "it felt" to speak from the pulpit. Some vague fancies were stirring in me, that I could speak if I had the chance; very vague they were, for the notion that I might ever speak on the platform had never dawned on me; only the longing to find outlet in words was in me; the feeling that I had something to say, and the yearning to say it. So, queer as it may seem, I ascended the pulpit in the big, empty, lonely church, and there and then I delivered my first lecture! I shall never forget the feeling of power and of delight which came upon me as my voice rolled down the aisles, and the passion in me broke into balanced sentences, and never paused for rhythmical expression, while I felt that all I wanted was to see the church full of upturned faces, instead of the emptiness of the silent pews. And as though in a dream, the solitude became peopled, and I saw the listening faces and the eager eyes, and as the sentences came unbidden from my lips, and my own tones echoed back to me from the pillars of the ancient church, I knew of a verity that the gift of speech was mine, and that if ever, and it seemed then so impossible, if ever the chance came to me of public work, that at least this power of melodious utterance should win hearing for any message I had to bring.

But that knowledge remained a secret all to my own self for many a long month, for I quickly felt ashamed of that foolish speechifying in an empty church, and I only recall it now because, in trying to trace out one's mental growth, it is only fair to notice the first silly striving after that expression in spoken words, which, later, has become to me one of the deepest delights of life.

MRS. FRANCES TROLLOPE

Mrs. Frances Trollope traveled to America in 1827 and wrote of her observations in Domestic Manners of the Americans. *She describes here a lecture she hears by Fanny Wright.*

That a lady of fortune, family, and education, whose youth had been passed in the most refined circles of private life, should present herself to the people as public lecturer, would naturally excite surprise anywhere, and the *nil admirari* of the old world itself would hardly be sustained before such a spectacle; but in America, where women are guarded by a seven-fold shield of insignificance, it caused an effect that can hardly be described. "Miss Wright, of Nashoba, is going to lecture at the court-house" sounded from street to street and from house to house. I shared the surprise, but not the wonder; I knew her extraordinary gift of eloquence, her almost unequal command of words, and the wonderful power of her rich and thrilling voice; and I doubted not that if it were her will to do it, she had the power of commanding the attention, and enchanting the ear of any audience before whom it was her pleasure to appear. I was most anxious to hear her, but was almost deterred from attempting it by the reports of the immense crowd that was expected. After many consultations, and after hearing that many other ladies intended going, my friend, Mrs. P., and myself decided upon making the attempt, accompanied by a party of gentlemen, and found the difficulty less than we anticipated, though the building was crowded in every part. We congratulated ourselves that we had the courage to be among the number, for all my expectations fell far short of the splendor, the brilliance, the overwhelming eloquence of this extraordinary orator.

Her lecture was upon the nature of true knowledge, and it contained little that could be objected to, by any sect or party; it was intended as an introduction to the strange and starling theories contained in her subsequent lectures and could harm only by the hints it contained that the fabric of human wisdom could rest securely on no other base than that of human knowledge.

But to return to Miss Wright—it is impossible to imagine anything more striking than her appearance. Her tall and majestic figure, the deep and almost solemn expression of her eyes, the simple contour of her finely formed head, unadorned, excepting by its own natural ringlets; her garment of plain white muslin, which hung around her in folds that recalled the drapery of a Grecian Statue, all contributed to produce an effect, unlike anything I had ever seen before, or ever expect to see again.

I shall never forget the experience.

ELIZA LYNN LINTON

Eliza Lynn Linton was the first salaried woman journalist in England and became a prominent critical voice attacking the "unfeminine" women rebellion had produced; in fact, her article in Saturday Review *coined the phrase "girl of the period" that became familiar in jokes, cartoons, and products. In this 1868 article, she accuses upper-middle-class girls of acting like prostitutes.*

Time was when the phrase "a fair young English girl" meant the ideal of womanhood, a girl who could be trusted alone if need be, because of the innate purity and dignity of her nature, but who was neither bold in bearing nor masculine in mind; a girl who, when she married, would be her husband's friend and companion, but never his rival; one who would consider his interests as identical with her own, and not hold him as just so much fair game for spoil; who would make his house his true home and place of rest, not a mere passage-place for vanity and ostentation to pass through; a tender mother, an industrious housekeeper, a judicious mistress to her servants.

This was in the old time when girls were content to be as God and nature had made them. Of late years we have changed the pattern, and have given to the world a race of women as utterly unlike the old insular ideal as if we had created another nation altogether.

The girl of the period is a creature who dyes her hair and paints her face, a creature whose sole idea of life is fun; whose sole aim is unbounded luxury; and whose dress is the chief object of such thought and intellect as she possesses. Her main endeavor is to outvie her neighbors in the extravagance of fashion.

This imitation of the *demi-monde* in dress leads to something in manner and feeling, not quite so pronounced perhaps, but far too like to be honorable to herself or satisfactory to her friends. It leads to slang, bold talk, and general fastness; to the love of pleasure and indifference to duty; to the desire of money before either love or happiness; to uselessness at home, dissatisfaction with the monotony of ordinary life, horror of all useful work; in a word, to the worst forms of luxury and selfishness—to the most fatal effects arising from want of high principle and absence of tender feeling.

No one can say of the modern English girl that she is tender, loving, retiring, or domestic. The legal barter of herself for so much money, representing so much dash, so much luxury and pleasure—that is her idea of marriage, the only idea worth entertaining. For all seriousness of thought respecting the duties or the consequences of marriage, she has not a trace.

If children come, they find but a stepmother's cold welcome from her, and if her husband thinks that he has married anything that is to belong to him, the sooner he wakes from his hallucination, the less severe will be his disappointment. She has married his house, his carriage, his balance at the banker's, his title; and he himself is just the inevitable condition clogging the wheel of her fortune; at best an adjunct, to be tolerated with more or less patience as may chance.

But the girl of the period does not marry easily. Men are afraid of her; and with reason. They may amuse themselves with her for an evening, but they do not readily take her for life. Besides, after all her efforts, she is only a poor copy of the real thing; and the real thing is far more amusing than the copy, because it is real. Men can get that whenever they like; and when they go into their mothers' drawing-rooms, with their sisters and their sisters' friends, they want something of quite a different flavor.

GIORGIONE WILLOUGHBY

The character of Giorgione Willoughby comes through quite clearly in the following monologue entitled "Flower O' the Peach" in Harriet Prescott Spofford's "The Amber Gods" (The Atlantic Monthly, January and February1860).

We've some splendid old point-lace in our family, yellow and fragrant, loose-meshed. It isn't everyone has point at all; and of those who have, it isn't everyone can afford to wear it. I can. Why? O, because it's in character. Besides, I admire point any way—it's so becoming. And then, you see, this amber! Now what is in finer unison, this old point-lace, all tags and tangle and fibrous and bewildering, and this amber, to which heaven knows how many centuries, maybe, with all their changes, brought perpetual particles of increase? I like yellow things, you see.

To begin at the beginning. My name, you're aware, is Giorgione Willoughby. Queer name for a girl! Yes; but before Papa sowed his wild-oats, he was one afternoon in Fiesole, looking over Florence nestled below, when some whim took him to go into a church there, a quiet place, full of twilight and one great picture, nobody within but a girl and her little salve—the one watching her mistress, the other saying dreadfully devout prayers on an amber rosary, and of course she didn't see him, or didn't appear to. After he got there, he wondered what on Earth he came for, it was so dark and poky, and he began to feel uncomfortable—when all of a sudden a great ray of sunset dashed through the window, and drowned the place in the splendor of the window, and drowned the place in the splendor of the illumined painting. Papa adores rich colors; and he might have been satiated here, except that such things make you want more. It was a Venus— no, though, it couldn't have been a Venus in a church, could it? Well, then, a Magdalen, I guess, or a Madonna, or something, I fancy the man painted for himself, and christened for others. So, when I was born, some years afterward, Papa, gratefully remembering this dazzling little vignette of his youth, was absurd enough to christen *me* Giorgione. That's how I came by my identity; but the folks all call me Yone—a baby name.

I'm a blonde, you know—none of your silver-washed things. I wouldn't give a *fico* for a girl with flaxen hair; she might as well be a wax doll, and have her eyes moved by a wire; besides, they've no souls. I imagine they were remnants at *our* creation, and somehow scrambled together, and managed to get up a little life among themselves; but it's good for nothing, and everybody sees through the pretense. They're glass chips, and brittle shavings, slender pinkish scrids—no name for them; but just you say "blonde," soft and slow and rolling, it brings up a brilliant, golden vitality, all manner of white and torrid magnificences, and you see me! I've watched little bugs—gold rose-chafers—lie steeping in the sun, till every atom of them must have been searched with the warm radiance, and have felt that, when they reached that point, I was just like them, golden all through—not dyed, but created. Sunbeams like to follow me, I think. Now, when I stand in one before this glass, infiltrated with the rich tinge, don't I look like the spirit of it just stepped out for inspection? I seem to myself like the complete incarnation of light, full, bounteous, overflowing, and I wonder at and adore anything so beautiful; and the reflection grows finer and deeper while I gaze, till I dare not do so any longer. So, without more words, I'm a golden blonde. You see me now: not too tall—five feet four; not slight, or I couldn't have such perfect roundings, such flexible moulding. Here's nothing of the spiny Diana and Pallas, but Clytie or Isis speaks in such delicious curves. It doesn't look like flesh and blood, does it? Can you possibly imagine it will ever change? Oh!

Now see the face—not small, either; lips with no particular out-line, but melting, and seeming as if they would stain yours, should you touch them. No matter about the rest, except the eyes. Do you meet such eyes often? You wouldn't open yours so if you did. Note their color now, before the ray goes. Yellow hazel! Not a bit of it! Some folks say topaz, but they're fools. Nor sherry. There's a dark sardine base, but over it real seas of light, clear light; there isn't any positive color; and once when I was angry, I caught a glimpse of them in a mirror, and they were quite white, perfectly colorless, only luminous. I looked like a fiend, and, you may be sure, recovered my temper directly—easiest thing in the world, when you've motive enough. You see the pupil is small, and that gives more expansion and force to the iris; but sometimes in an evening, when I'm too gay, and a true damask settles in the cheek, the pupil grows larger and crowds out the light, and under these thick brown lashes, these yellow-hazel eyes of yours, they are dusky and purple and deep with flashes, like pansies lit by fire-flies, and then common folks call them black. Be sure, I've never got such eyes for nothing, any more than this hair. That is Lucrezia Borgian, spun gold, and ought to take the world in its toils. I always wear these thick, riotous curls 'round my temples and face; but the great braids behind—O, I'll uncoil them, before my toilet is over.

There, now! You're perfectly shocked to hear me go on so about myself; but you oughtn't to be. It isn't lawful for anyone else, because praise is intrusion; but if the rose please to open her heart to the moth, what then? You know, too, I didn't make myself; it's no virtue to be so fair. I'm not good, of course; I wouldn't give a fig to be good. So it's not vanity. It's on a far grander scale; a splendid selfishness—authorized, too; and Papa and Mamma brought me up to worship beauty—and there's the fifth commandment, you know.

MARY SOMERVILLE

Mary Somerville (1791–1813) grew up in Scotland; her work as a mathematical astronomer influenced the teaching and practice of the physical sciences in America and England; she also set the standard for modern scientific writing. Getting an education, however, was not easy as she describes in her Personal Recollections. *After receiving what was considered an adequate education for girls ("it was thought sufficient for the girls to be able to read the Bible; very few even learnt to write"), Somerville was sent to an academy for girls, Nasmyth.*

Nasmyth, an exceedingly good landscape painter, had opened an academy for ladies in Edinburgh, a proof of the gradual improvement which was taking place in the education of the higher classes; my mother very willingly allowed me to attend it. Mr. Nasmyth, besides being a very good artist, was clever, well-informed, and had a great deal of conversation. One day I happened to be near him while he was talking to the Ladies Douglas about perspective. He said, "You should study Euclid's *Elements of Geometry*; the foundation not only of perspective, but of astronomy and all mechanical science." Here, in the most unexpected manner, I got the information I wanted, for I at once saw that it would help me to understand some parts of Robertson's *Navigation*; but as to going to a bookseller and asking for Euclid, the thing was impossible! Besides, I did not yet know anything definite about algebra, so no more could be done at that time; but I never lost sight of an object which had interested me from the first.

On returning to Burntisland, I played on the piano as diligently as ever, and painted several hours every day. At this time, however, a Mr. Craw came to live with us as tutor to my youngest brother, Henry. He had been educated for the kirk [church], was a fair Greek and Latin scholar, but, unfortunately for me, was no mathematician. He was a simple, good-natured kind of man, and I ventured to ask him about algebra and geometry, and begged him, the first time he went to Edinburgh, to buy me something elementary on these subjects, so he soon brought me *Euclid* and Bonnycastle's *Algebra*, which were the books used in the schools at that time. Now I had got what I so long and earnestly desired. I asked Mr. Craw to hear me demonstrate a few problems in the first book of *Euclid*, and then I continued the study alone with courage and assiduity, knowing I was on the right road.

I had to take part in the household affairs, and to make and mend my own clothes. I rose early, played on the piano, and painted during the time I could spare in the daylight hours, but I sat up very late reading Euclid. The servants, however, told my mother, "It was no wonder the stock of candles was soon exhausted, for Miss Mary sat up reading till a very late hour"; whereupon an order was given to take away my candle as soon as I was in bed. I had, however, already gone through the first six books of *Euclid*, and now I was thrown on my memory, which I exercised by beginning at the first book, and demonstrating in my mind a certain number of problems every night, till I could nearly go through the whole. My father came home for a short time, and, somehow or other, finding out what I was about, said to my mother, "Peg, we must put a stop to this, or we shall have Mary in a strait jacket one of these days. There was X., who went raving mad about the longitude!"

So I was forced to discontinue my studies. After the death of my husband, however, I took them up again with enthusiasm.

DR. ELIZABETH GARRETT ANDERSON

*In responding to an article by Dr. Henry Maudsley that claimed
menstruation was a disability, Dr. Elizabeth Garrett Anderson
(1836–1917), who founded the New Hospital for Women in 1882, refutes him strongly.*

When we are told that in the labor of life women cannot disregard
their special physiological functions without danger to health, it is
difficult to understand what is meant, considering that in adult life
healthy women do as a rule disregard them almost completely. It is,
we are convinced, a great exaggeration to imply that women of average health are periodically incapacitated from serious work by the
facts of their organization. Among poor women, where all the avail-
able strength is spent upon manual labor, the daily work goes on
without intermission, and, as a rule, without ill effects. For example,
do domestic servants, either as young girls or in mature life, show by
experience that a marked change in the amount of work expected
from them must be made at these times unless their health is to be in-
jured? It is well known that they do not.

  If we had no opportunity of measuring the attainments of ordinary
young men, or if they really were the intellectual athletes Dr.
Maudsley's warnings would lead us to suppose them to be, the question, "Is it well for women to contend on equal terms with men for
the goal of man's ambition?" might be as full of solemnity to us as it
is to Dr. Maudsley. As it is, it sounds almost ironical. Hitherto, most
of the women who have "contended with men for the goal of man's
ambition" have had no chance of being any the worse for being allowed to do so on equal terms. They have had all the benefit of being
heavily handicapped. Over and above their assumed physical and
mental inferiority, they have had to start in the race without a great
part of the training men have enjoyed, or they have gained what

training they could in an atmosphere of hostility, to remain in which has taxed their strength and endurance far more than any amount of actual mental work could tax it. Would, for instance, the ladies who for five years have been trying to get a medical education at Edinburgh find their task increased, or immeasurably lightened, by being allowed to contend "on equal terms with men" for that goal?

Even were the dangers of continuous mental work as great as Dr. Maudsley thinks they are, the dangers of a life adapted to develop only the specially and consciously feminine side of the girl's nature would be much greater. From the purely physiological point of view, it is difficult to believe that study much more serious than that usually pursued by young men could do a girl's health as much harm as a life directly calculated to over-stimulate the emotional and sexual instincts, and to weaken the guiding and controlling forces which these instincts so imperatively need. The stimulus found in novel-reading, in the theater and ballroom, the excitement which attends a premature entry into society, the competition of vanity and frivolity, these involve far more real dangers to the health of young women than the competition for knowledge, or for scientific or literary honors, ever has done, or is ever likely to do. And even if, in the absence of real culture, dissipation be avoided, there is another danger still more difficult to escape, of which the evil physical results are scarcely less grave, and this is dullness. There is no tonic in the pharmacopoeia to be compared with happiness, and happiness worth calling such is not known where the days drag along filled with make-believe occupations and dreary sham amusements. Thousands of young women, strong and blooming at eighteen, become gradually languid and feeble under the depressing influence of dullness, not only in the special functions of womanhood, but in the entire cycle of the processes of nutrition and enervation, till in a few years they are morbid and self-absorbed, or even hysterical. If they had had upon leaving school some solid intellectual work which demanded real thought and excited general interest, and if this interest had been helped by the stimulus of an examination, in which distinction would have been a legitimate source of pride, the number of such cases would probably be indefinitely smaller than it is now. Moreover, by entering society at a somewhat less immature age, a young woman is more able to take an intelligent part in it; is prepared to get more real pleasure from the companionship it affords, and, suffering less from *ennui*, she is less apt to make a hasty and foolish marriage. From the physiological point of view, a change in the arrangements of young women's lives which tends to discourage very early marriages will probably do more for their health and for the health of their children than any other change could do.

MRS. LITTLE

In the following account of a runaway slave, physical and psychological hardships are described. Mrs. Little was seventeen years old when she ran away from Tennessee, where she was a field hand. The account was published in 1855 from an interview.

My shoes gave out before many days—then I wore my husband's old shoes till they were used up. Then we came on barefooted all the way to Chicago. My feet were blistered and sore and my ankles swollen, but I had to keep on. There was something behind me driving me. At the first water we came to I was frightened. It was a swift but shallow stream. I felt afraid at getting into the boat to cross the Ohio River. I had never been in any boat whatever. "John," said I, "don't you think we'll drown?" "I don't care if we do," said he.

We never slept at the same time: while one slept, the other kept watch, day or night. At Cairo, the gallinippers [mosquitoes] were so bad, we made a smoke to keep them off. Soon after I heard a steamboat bell tolling. Presently there she was, a great boat full of white men. We were right on the river's bank, and our fire sent the smoke straight up. Presently they saw our fire, and hailed, "Boat ashore! boat ashore! runaway niggers!" We put out our fire and went further back from the river, but the mosquitoes were so bad, we made another fire. But a man with a gun then came along, looking up into the trees. I scattered the fire to put it out, but it smoked so much the worse. We at last hid in a thicket of briers, where we were almost devoured by mosquitoes for want of a little smoke.

One morning, being on a prairie where we could see no house, we ventured to travel by day. We encountered an animal, which we at first supposed to be a dog; but when he came near, we concluded it to be a wolf. We went on, and then we saw three large wood wolves, sneaking around as if waiting for darkness. As we kept on, the three wolves kept in sight, now on one hand, now on the other. I felt afraid, expecting they would attack us, but they left us. Afterward we made a fire with elder stalks, and I undertook to make some corn bread. I got it mixed, and put it on the fire—when I saw a party of men and boys on horseback, apparently approaching us. I put out the fire; they turned a little away and did not appear to perceive us. I rekindled the fire and baked our bread. We used to laugh to think how people would puzzle over who drank the milk and left the pitchers and who hooked the dough.

I never will forget that time.

MRS. BURROWS

Mrs. Burrows wrote this account for her Cooperative Guild of her childhood in field work.

In the very short schooling that I obtained, I learned neither grammar nor writing. On the day that I was eight years of age, I left school and began to work fourteen hours a day in the fields, with from forty to fifty other children of whom, even at that early age, I was the eldest. We were followed all day long by an old man carrying a long whip in his hand, which he did not forget to use. A great many of the children were only five years of age. You will think that I am exaggerating, but I am *not*; it is as true as the Gospel. Thirty-five years ago is the time I speak of, and the place, Croyland in Lincolnshire, nine miles from Peterborough. I could even now name several of the children who began at the age of five to work in the gangs, and also the name of the ganger.

We always left the town, summer and winter, the moment the old Abbey clock struck six. We had to walk a very long way to our work, never much less than two miles each way, and very often five miles each way. The large farms all lay a good distance from the town, and it was on those farms that we worked. In the winter, by the time we reached our work, it was light enough to begin, and of course we worked until it was dark and then had our long walk home. I never remember to have reached home sooner than six and more often seven, even in winter.

In all the four years I worked in the fields, I never worked one hour under cover of a barn, and only once did we have a meal in a house. And I shall never forget that one meal or the woman who gave us it. It was a most terrible day. The cold east wind (I suppose it was an east wind, for surely no wind ever blew colder), the sleet and snow which came every now and then in showers seemed almost to cut us to pieces. Croyland and Peterborough. Had the snow and sleet come continuously, we should have been allowed to come home, but because it only came at intervals, of course we had to stay. Dinnertime came, and we were preparing to sit down under a hedge and eat our cold dinner and drink our cold tea, when we saw the shepherd's wife coming towards us, and she said to our ganger, "Bring these children into my house and let them eat their dinner there." We went into that very small two-roomed cottage, and when we got into the largest room, there was not standing room for us all, but this woman's heart was large, even if her house was small, and so she put her few chairs and table out into the garden, and then we all sat down in a ring upon the floor. She then placed in our midst a very large saucepan of hot boiled potatoes, and bade us help ourselves. Truly, although I have attended scores of grand parties and banquets since that time, not one of them has seemed half as good to me as that meal did.

For four years, summer and winter, I worked in these gangs—no holidays of any sort, with the exception of very wet days and Sundays—and at the end of that time it felt like heaven to me when I was taken to the town of Leeds and put to work in a factory.

A VARGANT WOMAN

Henry Mayhew (1812-1887), a journalist, had a fascination with what we now call oral history. He went about the streets of nineteenth century London observing and talking to the people he saw there and reporting his conversations in daily newspapers and in a book, London and the London Poor *(1862) from which the following account is taken. The woman it a vagrant, and she tells a story similar to some runaways' stories today.*

I went to the shirt-making when I was twelve years of age, and that used to bring me about four quid a day, and with that I used to buy my bread, for we never got a halfpenny from my father to keep us. The young chap that I first took up with was a carpenter. He was apprenticed to the trade. He enticed me away. He told me that if I'd come to London with him, he'd do anything for me. I used to tell him how badly my father treated me, and he used to tell me not to stop at home. I have been knocking about three years, and I'm twenty now, so I leave you to say how old I was then. No, I can't say. I never learnt my ciphering.

I hadn't many clothes when I left my father's home. I had nothing but what I stood upright in. I had no more clothes when I was at home. When my young man left me, there was another young girl in the lodging-house who advised me to turn out upon the streets. I went and took her advice. I did like the life for a bit, because I see'd there was money getting by it. Sometimes I got four shillings a day, and sometimes more than that. There were a lot of girls like me at the same house. No tramps used to come there, only young chaps and gals that used to go out thieving. My young man didn't thieve, not while he was with me, but I did afterwards. I've seen young chaps brought in there by the girls merely to pay their lodging money. The landlady told us to do that. We used to be all in the same room, chaps and girls, sometimes nine or ten couples in the same room—only little bits of girls and chaps. I have seen girls there twelve years of age. The boys was about fifteen or sixteen. They used to swear dreadful.

I had one fancy-man. He was a shoplifter and a pickpocket: he has got two years now. I went to see him once in quod; some calls it "The Steel!" I cried a good deal when he got nailed, sir: I loved him. I saw I couldn't get him off, 'cause it was for a watch, and the gentleman went so hard against him. I was with him at the time he stole it, but I didn't know he'd got it till I saw him run. I got the man down by sawmill; he was tipsy. He was a gentleman, and said he would give me five shillings if I would come along with him. My fancy-man always kept near to me whenever I went out at night. I wasn't to go out to take the men home; it was only to pick them up. My young man used to tell me how to rob the men. I'd get them in a corner, and then I used to take out of their pockets whatever I could lay my hands on; and then I used to hand it over to him, and he used to take the things home and "fence" them. We used to do a good deal this way sometimes: often we'd get enough to keep us two or three days. At last he got caught for the watch; and when I see'd I couldn't get him off, I went down into the country—down into Essex, sir.

I shouldn't like to give it up just yet. I do like to be in the country in the summertime. I like haymaking and hopping, because that's a good bit of fun. Still, I'm sick and tired of what I'm doing now. It's the winter that sickens me. I'm worn out now, and I often sits and thinks of the life that I've led. I think of my kind, dear mother, and how good I would have been if my father had taught me better. Still, if I'd clothes, I'd not give up my present life. I'd be down in the country now. I do love roving about, and I'm wretched when I'm not at it.

ELIZABETH DICKSON

In 1867, Elizabeth Dickson, a widow with eleven children, tells why she sent her children out to work and how hard the work was.

What I say is, these gangs should not be as they are. Sometimes the poor children are very ill-used by the gangmaster. One has used them horribly, kicking them, hitting them with fork handles, hurdlesticks, etc., and even knocking them down. I have many a time seen my own and other children knocked about. It is if the children play and don't mind their work, or are a little troublesome anyways, or he has set them more than they can do. You see, their little spirits get so high, and they will talk to the last, and that is aggravation. Sometimes, too, they cannot work properly because their hands are cut all across and blistered where they twist the stalk round to pull up the root. Of course he don't knock the big ones, it is the little ones he takes advantage of.

My children were obliged to go to work very young, some before they were seven years old. If you have nothing except what comes out of your fingers' end, as they say, it's no use, you must let them; they want more victuals.

My husband left me a widow with eleven children living, out of fifteen; nine of them being then under sixteen years old, and three under three years, two being twins. The parish allowed me three shillings, four pence in money and goods (bread) according to the number of children, but not widow's pay.

Jemima was not more than two moths, I think, over six years old when she went out. She said, "Mother, I want some boots to go to school," so I sent her out and saved up what she earned till it was enough to get them. She was a corpse from going in the turnips. She came home from work one day, when about ten and one-half years old, with dizziness and her bones aching and died and was buried and all in little better than a fortnight. The doctor said it was a violent cold stuck in her bones. Children stooping down get as wet at top as below. They get wet from the rain, too. Perhaps they may have to go out three or four times in a week and not earn two pence, not having made a quarter [of a day], and come home so soaked that the wet will run out of their things. I have often been obliged to take my flannel petticoat off and roll it round a girl's legs and iron it with a warming pan to take off the pain and misery of the bones and let her get to sleep. Some of the work is very hard, as pulling turnips and mangolds, muck shaking, and when turnips are being put into the ground, putting muck as fast as the plough goes along—work which women and girls have sometimes to do. Drawing mangolds is the hardest; globe mangolds are fit to pull your inside out, and you have often to kick them up. I have pulled till my hands have been that swelled that you can't see the knuckles on them. I have come home so exhausted that I have set down and cried; it would be an hour before I could pull my things off; and I have been obliged to have the table moved up to me because I could not move to it.

ELIZABETH STUART PHELPS

In the early twentieth century, Virginia Woolf describes her struggle to kill the angel in the house, an image she and other women have felt trapped by. In 1852, Elizabeth Stuart Phelps gives us an early image of that angel. A young wife, eager to continue her work after marriage and motherhood, is often distracted and prevented from doing it. Exhausted, she lies down one day and has the following dream.

Soon I found myself in a singular place. I was traveling a vast plain. No trees were visible, save those which skirted the distant horizon, and on their broad tops rested wreaths of golden clouds. Before me was a female, who was journeying towards that region of light. Little children were about her, now in her arms, now running by her side, and as they traveled, she occupied herself in caring for them. She taught them how to place their little feet—she gave them timely warnings of the pitfalls—she gently lifted them over the stumbling-blocks. When they were weary, she soothed them by singing of that brighter land, which she kept ever in view, and towards which she seemed hastening with her little flock. But what was most remarkable was that, all unknown to her, she was constantly watched by two angels, who reposed on two golden clouds which floated above her. Before each was a golden book and a pen of gold. One angel, with mild and loving eyes, peered constantly over right shoulder—another kept as strict a watch over her left. Not a deed, not a word, not a look, escaped their notice. When a good deed, word, look, went from her, the angel over the right shoulder, with a glad smile, wrote it down in his book; when an evil, however trivial, the angel over the left shoulder recorded it in his book—then with sorrowful eyes followed the pilgrim until he observed penitence for the wrong, upon which he dropped a tear on the record, and blotted it out, and both angels rejoiced.

To the looker-on, it seemed that the traveler did nothing which was worthy of such careful record. Sometimes she did but bathe the weary feet of her little children, but the angel *over the right shoulder* wrote it down. Sometimes she did but patiently wait to lure back a little truant who had turned his face away from the distant light, but the angel *over the right shoulder* wrote it down. Sometimes she did but soothe an angry feeling or raise a drooping eyelid, or kiss away a little grief; but the angel *over the right shoulder* wrote it down.

Sometimes, her eye was fixed so intently on that golden horizon, and she became so eager to make progress thither, that the little ones, missing her care, did languish or stray. Then it was that the angel *over the left shoulder* lifted his golden pen and made the entry, and followed her with sorrowful eyes until he could blot it out. Sometimes she seemed to advance rapidly, but in her haste the little one had fallen back, and it was the sorrowing angel who recorded her progress. Sometimes so intent was she to gird up her loins and have her lamp trimmed and burning that the little children wandered away quite into forbidden paths, and it was the angel *over the left shoulder* who recorded her diligence.

Now as I looked, I felt that this was a faithful and true record, and was to be kept to that journey's end. The strong clasp of gold on those golden books also impressed me with the conviction that when they were closed, it would only be for a future opening.

My sympathies were warmly enlisted for the gentle traveler, and with a beating heart, I quickened my steps that I might overtake her. I wished to tell her of the angels keeping watch above her—to entreat her to be patient and faithful to the end—for her life's work was all written down—every item of it—and the *results* would be known when those golden books should be unclasped.

I wished to beg of her to think no duty trivial which must be done, for over her right shoulder and over her left were recording angels who would surely take note of all!

Eager to warn the traveler of what I had seen, I touched her. The traveler turned, and I recognized or seemed to recognized *myself.* Startled and alarmed, I awoke in tears.

MRS. MALLARD

Kate Chopin's The Story of an Hour *(1894) tells the story of a wife, Mrs. Mallard, who is told that her husband has been killed in a train accident. Retreating to her room, the young wife grieves for her loss, but suddenly becomes aware of another feeling, a sense of freedom. Although she loved her husband, she felt oppressed in marriage, but had kept the feeling suppressed until now.*

When I had exhausted myself crying, I saw, outside my window, budding trees; suddenly a little whispered word escaped my slightly parted lips. I said it over and over under my breath: "free, free, free!" My pulses beat fast and the coursing blood warmed and relaxed every inch of my body.

I did not ask if it were or were not a monstrous joy that held me. A clear and exalted perception enabled me to dismiss the suggestion as trivial.

I knew that I would weep again when I saw the kind, tender hands folded in death; the face that had never looked save with love upon me, fixed and gray and dead. But I saw beyond that biter moment a long procession of years to come that would belong to me absolutely. And I opened and spread my arms out to them in welcome.

There would be no one to live for me in those coming years; I would live for myself. There would be no powerful will bending mine in that blind persistence with which men and women believe they have a right to impose a private will upon a fellow creature. A kind intention or a cruel intention made the act seem no less a crime as I looked upon it in that brief moment of illumination.

And yet I had loved him—sometimes. Often I had not. What did it matter! What could love, the unsolved mystery, count for in face of this possession of self-assertion which I suddenly recognized as the strongest impulse of my being!

"Free! Body and soul free!" I kept whispering.

Josephine was kneeling before the closed door with her lips to the keyhole, imploring for admission. "Louise, open the door! I beg; open the door—you will make yourself ill. What are you doing, Louise? For heaven's sake, open the door."

"Go away. I am not making myself ill." No; I was drinking in the very elixir of life through that open window.

My fancy was running riot along those days ahead of me. Spring days, and summer days, and all sorts of days that would be my own. I breathed a quick prayer that life might be long. It was only yesterday I had thought with a shudder that life might be long.

A JAPANESE WOMAN

Lafcadio Hearn, an American journalist, adopted Japan as his home, married a Japanese wife, became a Buddhist and teacher at the Imperial University, and translated the manuscript of a diary he received in 1900. He writes: "The brave resolve of the woman to win affection by docility and by faultless performance of duty, he gratitude for every small kindness, he childlike piety, her supreme unselfishness, her attempts to write poetry when her heart was breaking, I find touching but I do not find exceptional." The unnamed Japanese woman who marries a widower when she is twenty nine years old (an advanced age for marriage) describes her early days of marriage.

Even though the signs are unfavorable, I cannot postpone my marriage because I have already promised, I explained to my father, and I cannot now ask to have the day changed. As for the signs being unlucky, even though I should have to die on that account, I would not complain, for I should die in my own husband's house.

When the appointed day came, I had so much to do that I did not know how I should ever be able to get ready. And as it had been raining for several days, the roadway was very bad, which made matters worse for me—though, luckily, no rain fell on that day. I had to buy some little things; and I could not well ask mother to do anything for me—much as I wished for her help—because her feet had become very weak by reason of her great age. So I got up very early and went out alone and did the best I could; nevertheless, it was two o'clock in the afternoon before I got everything ready.

Then I had to go to the hairdresser's to have my hair dressed, and to go to the bath-house—all of which took time. And when I came back to dress, I found that no message had yet been received from Namiki-Shi, and I began to feel a little anxious. Just after we had finished supper, the message came. I had scarcely time to say good-by to all: then I went out—leaving my home behind forever—and walked with mother to the house of Okada-Shi, the matchmaker, and a family friend.

There I had to part even from mother; and the wife of Okada-Shi taking charge of me, I accompanied her to the house of Namiki-Shi, where the wedding ceremony was performed without any difficulty, and the time of the honorable leave-taking came more quickly than I had expected. When the guests all returned home, I felt very distressed.

Two or three days later, the father of my husband's former wife visited me and said: "Namiki-Shi is really a good man—a moral, steady man, but as he is also very particular about small matters and inclined to find fault, you had better always be careful to try to please him."

Now as I had been carefully watching my husband's ways from the beginning, I knew that he was really a very strict man, and I resolved so to conduct myself in all matters as never to cross his will.

The fifth day of the tenth month was the day for our first visit to my parents' house, and for the first time we went out together, but the weather suddenly became bad, and it began to rain. Then we borrowed a paper parasol, which we used as an umbrella, and though I was very uneasy lest any of my former neighbors should see us walking thus together, we luckily reached my parents' house and made our visit of duty without any trouble at all. While we were in the house, the rain fortunately stopped.

During this last month of the year, I made my spring robes for my husband and myself; then I learned for the first time how pleasant such work was, and I felt very happy. In fact, after we had visited a Shinto shrine and dined out together in a restaurant, I wrote this poem in my diary:

"Having been taken across the Imado-Ferry, I strangely met at the temple of Mimeguri-Inair with a person whom I had never seen before. Because of this meeting, our relation is now even more the relation of husband and wife. And my first anxious doubt, having passed away, my mind has become clear as the Sumida River. Indeed we are now like a pair of Miyako-birds (always together); and I ever think that I deserve to be envied . . . More than the pleasure of viewing a whole shore in blossom is the pleasure I now desire—always to dwell with this person, dearer to me than any flower, until we enter the White-Haired Temple. That we may so remain, I supplicate the Gods!"

So far we have never had any words between us nor any disagreement, and I have ceased to feel bashful when we go out visiting or sightseeing. Now each of us seems to think only of how to please the other, and I feel sure that nothing will ever separate us. May our relation always be thus happy!

ADRIENNE FARIVAL

In Lilacs *by Kate Chopin, Adrienne Farival, a young opera singer, retreats back to the convent of her youth every spring when she smells lilacs.*

Always shall I remember that morning as I walked along the boulevard with a heaviness of heart—oh, a heaviness which I hate to recall. Suddenly there was wafted to me the sweet odor of lilac blossoms. A young girl had passed me by, carrying a great bunch of them. Did you ever know, Sister Agathe, that there is nothing which so keenly revives a memory as a perfume—an odor?

Well, that is how it was with me, Sister Agathe, when the scent of the lilacs at once changed the whole current of my thoughts and my despondency. The boulevard, its noises, its passing throng, vanished from before my senses as completely as if they had been spirited away. I was standing here with my feet sunk in the green sward as they are now. I could see the sunlight glancing from that old white stone wall, could hear the notes of birds, just as we hear them now, and the humming of insects in the air. And through all I could see and could smell the lilac blossoms, nodding invitingly to me from their thick-leaved branches. It seems to me they are richer than ever this year, Sister Agathe. And do you know, I became like an *enragée*—nothing could have kept me back. I do not remember now where I was going; but I turned and retraced my steps homeward in a perfect fever of agitation: "Sophie! My little trunk—quick—the black one! A mere handful of clothes! I am going away. Don't ask me any questions. I shall be back in a fortnight." And every year since then it is the same. At the very first whiff of a lilac blossom, I am gone! There is no holding me back.

SARAH JOSEPHA HALE

Sarah Josepha Hale (1788–1879) became the editor of Godey's Lady's Book *in 1837 and remained editor for forty years. She influenced two generations of women and contributed to the segregation of women's sphere with pieces like the following, in which she claims a different role for women than for men.*

All that is truly good and beautiful in society, we owe to women. She, woman, was the *last work* of creation—the *last,* and therefore the *best*, in those qualities which raise human nature above animal life. She was not made to gratify man's sensual desires, but to refine his human affections and elevate his moral feelings. Endowed with superior beauty of person and a corresponding delicacy of mind, her soul was to "help" him where he was deficient—namely, in his spiritual nature.

Woman's spiritual strength seems perfected in her physical weakness.

Is not moral power better than mechanical invention?

Woman is the appointed preserver of whatever is good and pure and true in humanity. She is the first teacher. Every human being is submitted to her influence at the period when impressions take root and character receives its bias. Hence the condition of woman is the standard by which to estimate the true condition and character of the nation.

Every attempt to induce women to think they have a just right to participate in the public duties of government is injurious to their best interests and derogatory to their character. Our empire is purer, more excellent and spiritual.

AN OLDER WOMAN

Henry Mayhew, a journalist, describes his work, London Labour and
the London Poor, *as "the first attempt to publish the history of
people, from the lips of the people themselves." The following
account of a woman, sixty years old, who collects dog dung that is
used to clean leather tanyards, is one of those histories.*

I am sixty years of age. My father was a milkman, and very well off;
he had a barn and a great many cows. I was kept at school till I was
thirteen or fourteen years of age; about that time my father died, and
then I was taken home to help my mother in the business. After a
while, things went wrong—the cows began to die, and mother,
alleging she could not manage the business herself, married again. I
soon found out the difference. Glad to get away, anywhere out of the
house, I married a sailor, and was very comfortable with him for
some years as he made short voyages and was often at home, and always left me half his pay. At last he was pressed, when at home with
me, and sent away; I forget now where he was sent to, but I never
saw him from that day to this. I got some money that was due to him
from the India House, and, after that was all gone, I went into service, in the Mile-end Road.

There I stayed for several years, till I met my second husband,
who was bred to the water, too, but as a waterman on the river. We
did very well together for a long time, till he lost his health. He became paralyzed like, and was deprived of the use of all one side, and
nearly lost the sight of one of his eyes. Then we parted with everything we had in the world; and, at last, when we had no other means
of living left, we were advised to take to gathering pure [dog dung].
At first, I couldn't endure the business, I couldn't bear to eat a
morsel, and I was obliged to discontinue it for a long time. My husband kept at it, though, for he could do *that* well enough, only he

couldn't walk as fast as he ought. He couldn't lift his hands as high as his head, but he managed to work under him, and so put the pure in the basket. When I saw that he, poor fellow, couldn't make enough to keep up both, I took heart and went out again, and used to gather more than he did; that's fifteen years ago now—the time were good then, and we used to do very well.

If we only gathered a pail-full in the day, we could live very well; but we could do much more than that, for there wasn't near so many at the business then, and the pure was easier to be had. For my part, I can't tell where all the poor creatures have come from of late years; the world seems growing worse and worse and worse every day. They have pulled down the price of pure, that's certain; but the poor things must do something; they can't starve while there's anything to be got. Why, no later than six or seven years ago, it was as high as three shillings, six pence, and four farthings a pail-full, and a ready sale for as much of it as you could get; but now you can only get one shilling and in some places one shilling, two pence a pail-full; and, as I said before, there are so many at it that there is not much left for a poor old creature like me to find. The men that are strong and smart get the most, of course, and some of them do very well—at least they manage to live.

Six years ago, my husband complained that he was ill in the evening, and lay down in the bed—we lived in Whitechapel then. He took a fit of coughing and was smothered in his own blood. O dear, what troubles I have gone through! I had eight children at one time, and there is not one of them alive now. My daughter lived to thirty years of age, and then she died in childbirth, and, since then, I have had nobody in the wide world to care for me—none but myself, all alone as I am. After my husband's death, I couldn't do much, and all my things went away, one by one, until I've nothing left but bare walls, and that's the reason why I was vexed at first at your coming in, sir. I was yesterday out all day, and went round Aldgate,

Whitechapel, St. George's East, Stepney, Bow, and Bromley, and then came home; after that, I went over to Bermondsey, and there I got only six pence for my pains. Today I wasn't out at all; I wasn't well; I had a bad headache, and I'm so much afraid of the fevers that are all about here (though I don't know why I should be afraid of them). I was lying down, when you came, to get rid of my pains. There's such a dizziness in my head now, I feel as if it didn't belong to me. No, I have earned no money today. I have had a piece of dried bread that I steeped in water to eat. I haven't eat anything else today; but pray, sir, don't tell anybody of it. I could never bear the thought of going into the workhouse; I'm so used to the air that I'd sooner die in the street, as many I know have done. I've known several of our people who have sat down in the street with their basket alongside them and died. I knew one not long ago who took ill just as she was stooping down to gather up the pure and fell on her face; she was taken to the London Hospital and died at three o'clock in the morning. I'd sooner die like them than be deprived of my liberty and be prevented from going about where I liked.

A SHABBY YOUNG WOMAN

Early childhood experience may leave permanent scars. In Olive Schreiner's Undine, *a shabby young woman Undine meets on board a ship to South Africa, explains how she become involved with a married lover, and this account of a childhood experience may suggest a source for her sense of worthlessness and explain her vulnerability.*

I was always stupid; I think that must have been the reason why no one ever loved me. They sent me to school when I was quite a little child to see if it would do me any good, but I used to get so frightened I could never remember when we had to come up and say our lessons, and so I always stayed in the classes with the little girls. I think they used to like me, the very little ones; I could dress their dolls and even help them with their lessons a little.

You see, I was not stupid to them, but to the big girls—they could not bear me, but they used to let me darn their stockings for them and, when any of them got into a scrape, then they used to come to me and say, "Don't say it's not you if the teachers ask, because you are sure not to get a prize anyhow." And I used to say yes, because I thought it would make them love me; but it never did, it only made the teachers hate me.

One of them liked me, though—she always talked so softly to me; but one day when I was shut up all alone in the dark room that opened out of the schoolroom, I heard some of the teachers talking. I think they had forgotten me, and I heard them say I was the stupidest girl in the school and that they could not think how she could like me. "I do not like her," she said, "I feel sorry for her, she is such a poor thing; but there is not a girl in the school I care less about."

Then I lay down and cried. I had been so happy when I thought she loved me, and when I came out the girls all laughed at me because I had been crying, and said I was afraid of the dark (and I was not afraid at all—I liked it), but I did so want some one to help me, some one bigger and cleverer than I was.

Afterwards, when I grew a great girl, I left off trying to make people love me, because it was no use.

LITTLE WATERCRESS GIRL

In Street People of London *(1862), Henry Mayhew says the little watercress girl who gave the following statement was "only eight years of age but had entirely lost all childish ways, and was, indeed, in thoughts and manner, a woman. The poor child, Although the weather was severe, was dressed in a thin cotton gown, with a threadbare shawl wrapped round her shoulders. She wore no covering to her head, and the long rusty hair stood out in all directions. When she walked she shuffled along, for fear that the large carpet slippers that served her for shoes should slip off her feet."*

I go about the streets with watercresses, crying, "Four bunches a penny, watercresses." I am just eight years old—that's all—and I've a big sister and a brother and a sister younger than I am. On and off, I've been very near a twelvemonth in the streets.

Before that, I had to take care of a baby for my aunt. No, it wasn't heavy—it was only two month old; but I minded it for ever such a time—till it could walk. It was a very nice little baby, not a very pretty one; but, if I touched it under the chin, it would laugh.

Before I had the baby, I used to help mother, who was in the fur trade; and, if there was any slits in the fur, I'd sew them up. My mother learned me how to needlework and to knit when I was about five.

I used to go to school, too; but I wasn't there long. I've forgot about it now, it's such a time ago; and mother took me away because the master whacked me, though the missus use'n't to never touch me. I didn't like him at all. What do you think? He hit me three times, ever so hard, across the face with his cane, and made me go dancing down stairs; and when mother saw the marks on my cheek, she went to blow him up, but she couldn't see him—he was afraid. That's why I left school.

The cresses is so bad now that I haven't been out with 'em for three days. They're so cold, people won't buy 'em; for when I goes up to them, they say, "They'll freeze our bellies." Besides, in the market, they won't tell a ha' penny handful now—they're rist to a penny and tuppence. In summer, there's lots, an' most as cheap as dirt; but I have to be down at Farringdon-market between four and five, or else I can't get any cresses, because everyone almost—especially the Irish—is selling them, and they're picked up so quick. Some of the saleswomen—we never calls 'em ladies—is very kind to us children, and some of them altogether spiteful. The good ones will give you a bunch for nothing, when they're cheap; but the other, cruel ones, if you try to bate them a farthing less than, they ask you, will say, "Go along with you, you're no good."

It's very cold before winter comes on reg'lar—'specially getting up of morning. I gets up in the dark by the light of the lamp in the court. When the snow is on the ground, there's no cresses. I bears the cold—you must—so I puts my hands under my shawl, though it hurts 'em to take hold of the cresses, especially when we takes 'em to the pump to wash 'em. No; I never see any children crying—it's no use.

Sometimes I make a great deal of money. One day I took one shilling, six pence, and the cresses cost six pence; but it isn't often I get such luck as that. I oftener make three pence or four pence than one shilling; and then I'm at work, crying, "Cresses, four bunches a pence, cresses!" from six in the morning to about ten. The shops buy most of me. Some of 'em says, "Oh! I ain't a-going to give a pence for these," and they want 'em at the same price I buys 'em at.

I always give my mother my money, she's so very good to me. She don't often beat me; but, when she do, she don't play with me. She's very poor and goes out cleaning rooms sometimes; now she don't work at the fur [trade]. I ain't got no father, he's a father-in-law. No, mother ain't married again—he's a father-in-law. He grinds scissors, and he's very good to me. No, I don't mean by that he says kind things to me, for he never hardly speaks. When I gets home, after selling cresses, I puts the rooms to rights: mother don't make me do it, I does it myself. I cleans the chairs, though there's only two to clean. I takes a tub and scrubbing-brush and flannel and scrubs the floor—that's what I do three or four times a week.

KATE MARY EDWARDS

Kate Mary Edwards' memories of country-maids-of-all-work at the end of the century (1890).

It were nothing for a girl to be sent away to service when she were eleven year old. This meant leaving the family as she never been parted from for a day in her life afore, and going to some place miles away to be treated like something as ha'n't got as much sense or feeling as a dog. I'm got nothing against girls going into good service. In my opinion, good service in a properly run big house were a wonderful training for a lot o' girls who never would ha' seen anything different all the days o' their lives if they ha'n't a-gone. It were better than working on the land, then, and if it still existed now, I reckon I'd rather see any o' my daughters be a good housemaid or a well-trained parlourmaid than a dolled-up shop-assistant or a factory worker. Such gals as us from the fen di'n't get "good" service, though, not till we'd learnt a good deal the hard way. Big houses di'n't want little girls of eleven, even as kitchen maids, so the first few years 'ad to be put in somewhere else, afore you even got that amount o' promotion. Mostly they went to the farmers' houses within ten or twenty mile from where they'd bin born. These farmers were a jumped up, proud lot who di'n't know how to treat the people who worked for 'em. They took advantage o' the poor people's need to get their girls off their hands to get little for nearly nothing. The conditions were terrible.

I 'ad one friend as I were particular fond of, called for some reason as I never did know "Shady." She went to service when she were about thirteen, to a lonely outlaying fen farm in a place called Black-bushe. The house were a mile or more from the road, and there were no other house nearby. A big open farmyard were all 'round it on three sides, and at the back door, it opened straight into the main drain, about twelve feet wide and ten feet deep with sides like the wall of a house. There were no escape there.

She were woke up at 6:00 A.M. every morning by the horsekeeper, who had walked several mile to work already, and used a clothes prop to rattle on her window to rouse her. She had to get up straight away and light the scullery fire in the big, awkward old range, that she had on to get tea made for 6:30 A.M. for the horsekeeper, who baited his horses first, come in for his breakfast at six-thirty, and went out and yoked his horses so as to be away to work in the fields by seven o'clock. While the kettle boiled, she started to scrub the bare tiles o' the kitchen floor. This were a terrible job. There were no hot water, and the kitchen were so big there seemed nearly a acre of it to scrub—and when you'd finished that, there'd be the dairy, just as big and the scullery as well. Skirts were long an' got in the way as you knelt to scrub, and whatever you done you cou'n't help gettin' 'em wet. In the winter you'd only have the light o' candles to do it by, and the kitchen 'ould be so cold the water 'ould freeze afore you could mop it up properly.

ELIZA SOUTHGATE

In 1802, Eliza Southgate (1783–1809) describes a humorous scene that occurs in Portland one snowy evening about 3:00 A.M. after a night of dancing and card playing. In a playful tone, she shows some of the hardships of chivalry.

None but ladies were permitted to get into the carriage—it presently was stowed in so full that the horses could not move; the door was burst open, for such a clamor as the closing of it occasioned I never heard before.

The universal cry was "a gentleman in the coach, let him come out!"

We all protested there was none as it was too dark to distinguish; but the little man soon raised his voice and bid the coachman proceed; a dozen voices gave contrary orders.

'Twas a proper riot; I was really alarmed. My gentleman, with a vast deal of fashionable independence, swore no power on earth should make him quit his seat; but a gentleman at the door jump't into the carriage, caught hold of him, and would have dragged him out if we had not all entreated them to desist. He sqeezed again into his seat, and the carriage at length started full of ladies except our lady man, who had crept to us for shelter.

When we found ourselves in the street, the first thing was to find out who was in the carriage and when we were all going, who first must be left. Luckily, two gentlemen had followed by the side of the carriage, and when it stopped took out the ladies as they got to their houses.

Our sweet little, trembling, delicate, unprotected fellow sat immovable whilst the two gentlemen that were obliged to walk thro' all the snow and storm carried all the ladies from the carriage.

We at length arrived at the place of our destination. The gentle-men then proceeded to take us out. My beau, unused to carrying such a weight of sin and folly, sank under its pressure, and I was obliged to carry my mighty self through the snow, which almost buried me. Such a time: I never shall forget it!

SOJOURNER TRUTH

Sojourner Truth's famous "Ain't I a Woman?" speech still electrifies listeners.

Well, children, where there is so much racket, there must be something out of kilter. I think that 'twixt the Negroes of the South and the women at the North, all talking about rights, the white men will be in fix pretty soon. But what's all this here talking about?

That man over there says that women need to be helped into carriages, and lifted over ditches, and to have the best place everywhere. Nobody ever helps me into carriages, or over mud-puddles, or gives me any best place! And ain't I a woman? Look at me! Look at my arm. I have ploughed and planted, and gathered into barns, and no man could head me! And ain't I a woman? I could work as much and eat as much as a man—when I could get it—and bear the lash as well! And ain't I a woman? I have borne thirteen children, and seen them most all sold off to slavery, and when I cried out with my mother's grief, none but Jesus heard me! And ain't I a woman?

If the first woman God ever made was strong enough to turn the world upside down all alone, these women together ought to be able to turn it back, and get it right-side up again! And now they is asking to do it, the men better let them.

Obliged to you for hearing me, and now old Sojourner ain't got nothing more to say.

HETTY SORREL

In a prison cell, about to be hanged for murdering her newborn, Hetty Sorrel confesses to Dinah her guilt and describes the events that led up to this moment. In the darkness of a prison cell, Hetty's account of her desperate flight to find her lover who has deserted her, the sudden birth of her illegitimate child, her terror and panic, and the haunting cries of her newborn buried beneath the leaves chills the listener.

I came to a place where there was lots of chips and turf, and I sat down on the trunk of a tree to think what I should do. And all of a sudden I saw a hole under the nut tree, like a little grave. And it darted into me like lightning—I'd lay the baby there and cover it with the grass and chips. I couldn't kill it any other way. And I'd done it in a minute; and, O, it cried so—I *couldn't* cover it quite up—I thought perhaps somebody 'ud come and take care of it, and then it wouldn't die. And I made haste out of the wood, but I could hear it crying all the while; and when I got out into the fields, it was as if I was held fast—I couldn't go away, for all I wanted so to go. And I sat against the haystack to watch if anybody 'ud come: I was very hungry and I'd only a bit of bread left; but I couldn't go away. And after ever such a while—hours and hours—the man come, him in a smock-frock, and he looked at me so. I was frightened, and I made haste and went on. I thought he was going to the wood and would perhaps find the baby. And I went right on until I came to a village, a long way off from the wood; and I was very sick, and faint, and hungry. I heard the baby crying and thought the other folks heard it, too—and I went on. But I was so tired, and it was getting towards dark. And at last, by the roadside there was a barn—ever such a way off any house—like the barn in Abbot's Close; and I thought I could go in there and hide myself among the hay and straw, and nobody 'ud be likely to come. I went in, and it was half full o' trusses of straw, and there was some hay, too. And I made myself a bed, ever so far behind, where nobody could find me; and I was so tired and weak, I went to sleep . . . But, oh, the baby's crying kept waking me, and I thought that man as looked at me so was come and laying hold of me. But I must have slept a long while at last, though I don't know; for when I got up and went out of the barn, I didn't know whether it was night or morning. But it was morning, for it kept getting lighter, and I turned back the way I come. I couldn't help it—it was the baby's crying made me go, and yet I was frightened to death. I thought that man in the smock-frock 'ud see me and know I put the baby there. But I went on, for all that: I'd left off thinking about going home—it had gone out o' my mind. I saw nothing but that place in the wood where I'd buried the baby . . . I see it now. O shall I always see it?

I met nobody, for it was very early, and I got into the wood . . . I knew the way to the place . . . the place against the nut tree, and I could hear it crying at every step . . . I thought it was alive . . . I don't know if I was frightened or glad . . . I don't know what I felt. I only know I was in the wood and heard the cry. I don't know what I felt until I saw the baby was gone. And when I put it there, I thought I should like somebody to find it and save it from dying; but when I saw it was gone, I was struck like a stone, with fear. I never thought o' stirring, I felt so weak. I knew I couldn't run away, and everybody as saw me 'ud know about the baby. My heart went like a stone; I couldn't wish or try for anything. It seemed like as if I should stay there forever, and nothing 'ud ever change. But they came and took me away.

Do you think God will take away that crying and the place in the wood, now I've told everything?

EMMA SHEPPARD

Emma Sheppard, wife of a magistrate, wrote this description for a monthly magazine, Magdalen's Friend, *in 1860. She evokes a sympathetic portrait of her "fallen sister."*

English ladies, have you ever analyzed these two words—"a sister"—though "fallen"? Yes, high-born, gently bred, delicately nurtured Ladies, that poor Outcast, upon whom you cast an eye of scorn and loathing as perhaps she tramped up Regent Street this morning, looking wistfully at your luxurious carriage, with its warm wrappings from the cold, carrying you from shop to shop in quest of some small trifle—that poor, weary, outwardly hardened, sin-debased creature—a victim to man's brutal requirements—is, in the sight of our most holy God, your *sister*. Oh, think, the night after you read this, as you lie, perchance awake, and know that the husband of your youth, the children of your love, lie close by you—when the carpeted room, and the warm bed-hangings, and the ample coverings keep out a breath of the chilly, wintry air, which you think would kill you—think for ten minutes of midnight streets, cold pavements, dreary doorsteps, dark corners, on which, perhaps, the eye of God alone then looks—picture these filled with women, young girls, your sisters, once fair and loved as you, now debased and humbled and degraded to the level of the brutes, either cursing or drinking or quarreling, or following deeds of darkness such as your mind never *can* picture; and then turn your head on your pillow and bless that gracious God who has kept you *unfallen* in the eyes of the world.

In November 1858, my husband sent to prison, for the twenty-seventh time, a notorious offender, Matilda H., only twenty-nine, one of the most disorderly *habituées* of the streets. In jail, she found her first friend, the kind and earnest wife of the Governor of Shipton House of Correction, who spends much of her time among the female prisoners. Her kindly words gained influence over poor Matilda and secured her tender and most devoted love. After her term of imprisonment was over, the girl came back to Frome, determined to enter the workhouse, and, if possible, to bear the irksome and galling restraints there, and regain such a character as eventually to allow her to emigrate. *There* I visited her, giving her words of cheering purpose, getting the master of the workhouse to alter her work from oakum-picking (that degrading, unwomanly employment) to washing for the house and taking her up some tea and sugar now and then to soften the hardships I knew she was undergoing.

Christmas Eve 1858, when we took up our annual present to every member of the workhouse, I laid my hand on Matilda, after giving her her little packet, saying, "Be a good girl, and try to stay here." She beckoned me into a corner and took out of the bosom of her pauper dress a well-worn note, wrapped up in several scraps of paper, and tied with a bit of stocking cotton—her talisman—saying, "Here's what will keep me good—a note from that dear lady at the jail; I promise you, I won't vex her or you by being naughty."

Was there not here a touching revelation of a soft, tender heart in that rough, rude woman?

But Matilda again fell; the story too long to tell. After two months or more in the Workhouse, really behaving well, she asked leave one day to go out and see her mother, got drunk, returned to use violent language, etc., to the master, and was sent off for the twenty-eighth time to prison. My heart yearned over her. I drove over to Shipton, asked to see Matilda, and was shown alone into her cell. I laid my hand on her shoulder as we knelt side by side, and she shook like an earthquaking, with sobs of loving repentance. Then I offered her Clewer shelter. "Do let me see my old mother in Frome; she won't live over the two years I am away." I told her I could not trust her a night in Frome, but would arrange for her to come from Shipton by earliest train, March 31.

I returned to make these arrangements—bought some tea, sugar, bacon, etc., for the breakfast—the old parents whitewashed the tiny house in preparation. I went down to meet her at train by seven a.m., and about eleven, went up to her home. We read a few verses; then I prayed in the midst of the assembled family of parents, brothers, and sisters, and took her down to the station, so as to make *sure of* her. When I had taken her ticket for Windsor, I knew not where to put it for safety, so took off my own glove, put it on her, and placed the ticket inside. She looked at me wonderingly, then kissed the glove tenderly, with, "I'll *never* part with that as long as I live." What was this, but as loving a heart as yours or mine, for the first time called out into exercise?

If there was a heart in this poor, wretched, oft-convicted, scorned creature, why should we not seek and find the same in others?

CALAMITY JANE

Calamity Jane gave up her daughter shortly after birth because she couldn't raise her alone, but she kept in touch with the man who had adopted Janey and visited her a few times, never letting her know her true mother. She wrote her a series of letters that she never mailed, however; this one was written shortly after a visit East to see Janey.

O Janey, I did hate to come back here. Why couldn't I have stayed with you and Daddy Jim? Why didn't he ask me to stay? I was so in hope he would, but darling, your mother is a misfit in a home like you have—or what can be wrong? I had such a lovely time there. Why can't I ever be anybody worthwhile? I like will end up in the poor house in my old age. I am so discouraged. One consolation, I shall always know you are all right and I thank God for your Daddy Jim. I gave him ten thousand dollars to use for your education. There will be more in that old gambling tent for me when Luck again comes my way. I met Abbot on the street. He asked me for the price of a meal. I gave him my last fifty cents. My pocketbook looked so empty where only such a short while ago there could have been counted thousands that I tossed it out in the street. Abbot promised me a job in Deadwood, so I'm hitting the trail to that place soon. I'll never forget that party and will always think of you when I got my first glimpse of you that day, when your Daddy Jim called you in to meet me and when you asked me why I cried, and I told you that you reminded me of a little girl I once knew, and I told you of how she sailed away on a big ship and never came back to me and you said, "My Daddy Jim and I sail on big ships to cross the ocean lots of times. Once Mammy Ross and I went with him to Singapore, that's in China you know, and we gave the beggar children American gold, poor little starved things. Their clothes were all rags and I could see their ribs sticking out, and their hands were like little bird claws and their faces looked just like a starved kitten Daddy Jim's sailors found below in the steerage. I couldn't eat my dinner that night. They made me feel sick for their eyes were poked out."

Then your Daddy Jim left us alone. Remember, Janey? You told me about the women on your daddy's ship, and you mocked them making eyes at him. O, you were so comical then. When I asked you where your mother was, you said, "My mother is dead. She died a long time ago. She was Mother Helen O'Neil." I said, "O, I see," then it was that I held you close, Janey. It seemed for one moment I was back again with you in those terrible heart-breaking days in Yellow Stone Valley, facing life without your own Father, a future black and tragic for you, darling. Then your Daddy Jim came. I know God sent him to me. There I was in Omaha and watched the train carrying you away. Then that letter from Helen O'Neil, telling me you had gone out of my life forever, for they had gone to England. I thought that was the end, that I would never see you again. Then I was in your house in Virginia with you in my arms. You were such a little lady, darling. I have never seen a little girl with so many pretty dresses. O I shall always remember when I looked back after I got in the cab and saw your Daddy Jim take you by the hand and you both waved good-by till the horses turned the corner, shutting you from my sight. It will be years, so many of them, before I will ever see you again. Be good to Mammy Ross. She is so nice to you. That is what I wanted to tell you but didn't. There will never be for you the awful loneliness of empty years ahead, Janey, never as long as you have Mammy Ross and your Daddy Jim. How I wish I could say I had seen those countries where he has taken you. I hope you will think of me sometime and of the things I told you, so you would remember the woman your Daddy Jim called Jane and of the man I told you about we called Wild Bill Hickok. You said, "What a funny name," and when I showed you his picture, you said, "He isn't handsome like my Daddy Jim." There is nothing in this world quite so wonderful as the faith a child has in one they love. When you said your prayer that night to me, you added, "God bless Jane Hickok and that man who was shot in the back, wherever he is. Bless him because Jane loved him." I wondered how you knew that I loved him.

Good night, little girl, and may God keep you from all harm.

JANE WELSH CARLYLE

In 1859, Jane Welsh Carlyle, whose marriage to the demanding and often sickly writer Thomas Carlyle certainly was not ideally happy, speaks to a young friend on her engagement. As often happens, the "words of wisdom" the older woman offers the younger are likely to go unheeded.

And you are actually going to get married! You! Already! And you expect me to congratulate you! or "perhaps not." I admire the judiciousness of that "perhaps not." Frankly, my dear, I wish you all the happiness in the new life that is opening to you; and you are marrying under good auspices, since your father approves of the marriage. But congratulations on such occasions seems to me a tempting of providence. The triumphal-procession-air which, in our manners and customs, is given to marriage at the outset—that singing of *Te Deum* before the battle has begun—has, ever since I could reflect, struck me as somewhat senseless and somewhat impious. If ever one is to pray—if ever one is to feel grave and anxious—if ever one is to shrink from vain show and vain babble—surely it is just on the occasion of two human beings binding themselves to one another, for better and for worse, till death part them; just on that occasion which it is customary to celebrate only with rejoicings, and congratulations, and *trousseaux,* and white ribbon! Good God!

Will you think me mad if I tell you that when I read your words, "I am going to be married," I all but screamed? Positively, it took away my breath, as if I saw you in the act of taking a flying leap into infinite space. You had looked to me such a happy, happy little girl! Your father's only daughter; and he so fond of you, as he evidently was. After you had walked out of our house together that night, and I had gone up to my own room, I sat down there in the dark and took "a good cry." You had reminded me so vividly of my own youth, when I, also an only daughter—an only child—had a father as fond of me, as proud of me. I wondered if you knew your own happiness. Well! Knowing it or not, it has not been enough for you, it would seem. Naturally, youth is so insatiable of happiness, and has such sublimely insane faith in its own power to make happy and be happy.

MARGARET FULLER

Margaret Fuller (1810–1850), a feminist, a journalist, and a member of Emerson's intellectual circle in nineteenth-century Cambridge was always a radical, thinking about everything, not only about what was acceptable. Emerson, a lifelong friend, often wondered at her "violent" emotional life which she lived with "too much force of blood." In the following selection from her Memoirs, *she reflects on a subject much more common in the nineteenth century than today— women's love for other women.*

At Mr. G's, we looked over prints the whole evening, in peace. Nothing fixed my attention so much as a large engraving of Mme. Récamier in her boudoir. I have so often thought over the intimacy between her and Mme. DeStäel.

It is so true that a woman may be in love with a woman, and a man with a man. I like to be sure of it, for it is the same love which angels feel.

It is regulated by the same law as love between persons of different sexes; only it is purely intellectual and spiritual. Its law is the desire of the spirit to realize a whole, which makes it seek in another being the strong, the beautiful: the mute seek the eloquent, etc.; the butterfly settles always on the dark flower. Why did Socrates love Alcibiades? Why did Korner love Schneider? How natural is the love of Wallenstein for Mas; that of DeStäel for Récamier; mine for —. I loved —,for a time, with as much passion as I was then strong enough to feel. Her voice was always echoing in my ear; all poetic thoughts clustered round the dear image. This love was a key which unlocked for me many a treasure which I still possess; it was the carbuncle which cast light into so many of the darkest caverns of human nature. She loved me, too, though not so much, because her nature was "less high, less grave, less large, less deep." But she loved me more tenderly, less passionately. She loved me, for well I remember her suffering when first she could feel my faults, and knew one part of the exquisite veil rent away; how she wished to stay apart and weep the whole day.

I do not love her now with passion, but I still feel towards her as I can to no other woman. I thought of all this as I looked at Mme. Récamier.

CATHERINE EARNSHAW

Catherine Earnshaw, the heroine of Wuthering Heights, *describes her passionate attachment to Heathcliff, the beggar child her father brought home, and her decision to marry the wealthy Linton.*

If I were in heaven, I should be extremely miserable. I dreamt once that I was there. Heaven did not seem to be my home; and I broke my heart with weeping to come back to Earth; and the angels were so angry that they flung me out into the middle of the heath on the top of Wuthering Heights, where I woke sobbing for joy. That will do to explain my secret, as well as the other. I've no more business to marry Edgar Linton than I have to be in heaven; and if the wicked man in there had not brought Heathcliff so low, I shouldn't have thought of it. It would degrade me to marry Heathcliff now; so he shall never know how I love him: and that, not because he's hand-some, but because he's more myself than I am. Whatever our souls are made of, his and mine are the same; and Linton's is as different as a moonbeam from lightning, or frost from fire. Yet every Linton on the face of the earth might melt into nothing, before I could con-sent to forsake Heathcliff. Oh, that's not what I intend—that's not what I mean! I shouldn't be Mrs. Linton were such a price demanded! He'll be as much to me as he has been all his lifetime. Edgar must shake off his antipathy, and tolerate him, at least. He will, when he learns my true feelings towards him. Nelly, I see now, you think me a selfish wretch; but did it never strike you that if Heathcliff and I married, we should be beggars? Whereas, if I marry Linton, I can aid Heathcliff to rise, and place him out of my brother's power. I am marrying Linton for the sake of one who comprehends in his person my feelings to Edgar and myself. I cannot express it; but surely you and everybody have a notion that there is or should be an existence of yours beyond you. What were the use of my creation, if I were entirely contained here? My great miseries in this world have been Heathcliff's miseries, and I watched and felt each from the beginning: my great thought in living is himself. If all else perished, and *he* remained, I should still continue to be; and if all else remained, and he were annihilated, the universe would turn to a mighty stranger: I should not seem a part of it. My love for Linton is like the foliage in the woods: time will change it, I'm well aware, as winter changes the trees. My love for Heathcliff resembles the eternal rocks beneath: a source of little visible delight, but necessary. I *am* Heathcliff! He's always, always in my mind: not as, anymore than I am always a pleasure to myself, but as my own being. So don't talk of our separation again: it is impracticable.

SARAH PENN

In Mary Wilkins Freeman's The Revolt of Mother *(1891), Mother, Sarah Penn, has meekly lived all her married life in a cramped house and worked to help Father, Adoniram, run their farm. However, when Father begins to build a barn, Mother protests, standing in the doorway "like a queen" since "nobility of character manifests itself at loopholes when it is not provided with large doors." The previously uncomplaining Sarah demands to be heard as she drags Father about the few rooms in which she has had to live her married life.*

Now, Father, look here—I'm going to talk real plain to you; I never have since I married you, but I'm goin' to now. I ain't never complained, an' I ain't goin' to complain now, but I'm goin' to talk plain. You see this room here, Father—you look at it well. You see there ain't no carpet on the floor, an' you see the paper is all dirty an' droppin' off the walls. We ain't had no new paper on it for ten year, an' then I put it on myself, an' it didn't cost but nine pence a roll. You see this room, Father—it's all the one I've had to work in an' eat in an' sit in since we was married. There ain't another woman in the whole town whose husband ain't got half the means you have but what's got better. It's all the room Nanny's got to have her company in; an' there ain't one of her mates but what's got better, an' their fathers not so able as hers is. It's all the room she'll have to be married in. What would you have thought, Father, if we had had our weddin' in a room no better than this? I was married in my mother's parlor, with a carpet on the floor, an' stuffed furniture, an' a mahogany card table. An' this is all the room my daughter will have to be married in.

There, Father, there's all the room I've had to sleep in in forty year. All my children were born there—the two that died an' the two that's livin'. I was sick with a fever there.

Here is all the buttery I've got—every place I've got for my dishes, to set away my victuals in, an' to keep my milk pans in. Father, I've been takin' care of the milk of six cows in this place, an' now you're goin' to build a new barn, an' keep more cows, an' give me more to do in it.

There, Father, I want you to look at the stairs that go up to them two unfinished chambers that are all the places our son an' daughter have had to sleep in all their lives. There ain't a prettier girl in town nor a more ladylike one than Nanny, an' that's the place she has to sleep in. It ain't so good as your horse's stall; it ain't so warm an' tight.

Now, Father, I want to know if you think you're doin' right an' accordin' to what you profess. Here, where we was married, forty year ago, you promised me faithful that we should have a new house built in that lot over in the field before the year was out. You said you had money enough, an' you wouldn't ask me to live in no such place as this.

It is forty year now, an' you've been makin' more money, an' I've been savin' of it for you ever since, an' you ain't built no house yet. You've built sheds an' cow houses an' one new barn, an' now you're goin to build another. Father, I want to know if you think it's right. You're lodgin' your dumb beasts better than you are your own flesh an' blood. I want to know if you think it's right.

You can't say nothin' without ownin' it ain't right, Father. An' there's another thing—I ain't complained; I've got along forty year, an' I s'pose I should forty more, if it wa'n't for that—if we don't have another house, Nanny, she can't live with us after she's married. She'll have to go somewheres else to live away from us, an' it don't seem as if I could have it so, noways, Father. She wa'n't ever strong. She's got considerable color, but there wa'n't never any backbone to her. I've always took the heft of everything off her, an' she ain't fit to keep house an' do everything herself. She'll be all worn out inside of a year. Think of her doin' all the washin' an' ironin' an' bakin' with them soft white hands an' arms, an' sweepin'! I can't have it so, noways, Father.

Father, won't you think it over, an' have a house built there instead of a barn?

LINDSAY

The young woman, Lindsay, in The Story of an African Farm *by Olive Schreiner urges her lover, Waldo, to seek the worldly success denied her because she is a woman.*

That is no plan: travel—see the world—find work! If you go into the world aimless, without a definite object, dreaming—dreaming—you will be definitely defeated, bamboozled, knocked this way and that. In the end, you will stand with your beautiful life all spent and nothing to show. They talk of genius—it is nothing but this: that a man knows what he can do best, and does it, and nothing else. Waldo, I wish I could help you; I wish I could make you see that you must decide what you will be and do. It does not matter what you choose—be a farmer, businessman, artist, what you will—but know your aim, and live for that one thing. We have only one life. The secret of success is concentration; wherever there has been a great life, or a great work, that has gone before. Taste everything a little, look at everything a little; but live for one thing. Anything is possible to a man who knows his end and moves straight for it, and for it alone. I will show you what I mean: words are gas till you condense them into pictures.

Suppose a woman, young, friendless as I am, the weakest thing on God's earth. But she must make her way through life. What she would be she cannot be because she is a woman; so she looks carefully at herself and the world about her, to see where her path must be made. There is no one to help her; she must help herself. She looks. These things she has—a sweet voice, rich in subtle intonations; a fair, very fair face, with a power of concentrating in itself, and giving expression to, feelings that otherwise must have been dissipated in words; a rare power of entering into other lives unlike her own, and intuitively reading them aright. These qualities she has.

How shall she use them? A poet, a writer, needs only the mental; an artist needs an eye for form and color, and a musician an ear for time and tune, and the mere drudge has no need for mental gifts. But there is one art in which all she has would be used, for which they are all necessary—the delicate expressive body, the rich voice, the power of mental transposition. The actor, who absorbs and then reflects from himself other human lives, needs them all, but needs not much more. This is her end; but how to reach it? Before her are endless difficulties: she must be content to wait long before she can even get her feet upon the path. If she has made blunders in the past, if she has weighted herself with a burden which she must bear to the end, she must bear the burden bravely, and labor on. There is no use in wailing and repentance here: the next world is the place for that; this life is too short. By our errors we see deeper into life. They help us. If she does all this—if she waits patiently, if she is never cast down, never despairs, never forgets her end, moves straight towards it, bending men and things most unlikely to her purpose—she must succeed at last. Men and things are plastic—they part to the right and left when one comes among them moving in a straight line to one end. I know it by my own little experience. Long years ago, I resolved to be sent to school. It seemed a thing utterly out of my power; but I waited, I watched, I collected clothes, I wrote, took my place at the school. When all was ready, I bore with my full force on the Boer-woman, and she sent me at last. It was a small thing; but life is made up of small things, as a body is built up of cells.

ELIZABETH CADY STANTON

In 1860, Elizabeth Cady Stanton addressed the New York State legislature, asking them to release women from the "protection" of the law.

Just imagine an inhabitant of another planet entertaining himself some pleasant evening in searching over our great national compact, our Declaration of Independence, our Constitution, or some of our statute-books; what would he think of those "women and Negroes" that must be so fenced in, so guarded against? Why, he would certainly suppose we were monsters, like those fabulous giants or Brobdingnagians of olden times, so dangerous to civilized man, from our size, ferocity, and power. Then let him take up our poets, from Pope down to Dana; let him listen to our Fourth of July toasts, and some of the sentimental adultations of social life, and no logic could convince him that this creature of the law, and this angel of the family altar, could be one and the same being. Man is in such a labyrinth of contradictions with his marital and property rights; he is so befogged on the whole question of maidens, wives, and mothers that from pure benevolence we should relieve him from this troublesome branch of legislation. We should vote and make laws for ourselves. Do not be alarmed, dear ladies! You need spend no time reading Grotius, Coke, Puffendorf, Blackstone, Bentham, Kent, and Story to find out what you need. We may safely trust the shrewd selfishness of the white man and consent to live under the same broad code where he has so comfortably ensconced himself. Any legislation that will do for man, we may abide by most cheerfully.

Now do not think, gentlemen, we wish you to do a great many troublesome things for us. We do not ask our legislators to spend a whole session in fixing up a code of laws to satisfy a class of most unreasonable women. We ask no more than the poor devils in the

Scripture asked: "Let us alone." In mercy, let us take care of ourselves, our property, our children, and our homes. True, we are not so strong, so wise, so crafty as you are, but if any kind friend leaves us a little money, or we can by great industry earn fifty cents a day, we would rather buy bread and clothes for our children than cigars and champagne for our legal protectors. There has been a great deal written and said about protection. We, as a class, are tired of one kind of protection, that which leaves us everything to do, to dare, and to suffer, and strips us of all means for its accomplishment. We would not tax man to take care of us. No, the Great Father has endowed all his creatures with the necessary powers for self-support, self-defense, and protection. We do not ask man to represent us; it is hard enough in times like these for man to carry backbone enough to represent himself. So long as the mass of men spend most of their time on the fence, not knowing which way to jump, they are surely in no condition to tell us where we had better stand. In pity for man, we would no longer hang like a mill-stone round his neck. Undo what man did for us in the Dark Ages and strike out all special legislation for us; strike the words "white male" from all your constitutions, and then, with fair sailing, let us sink or swim, live or die, survive or perish together.

LOUISA MAY ALCOTT

Louisa May Alcott, author of Little Women, *describes her duties at a Civil War hospital.*

Up at six, dress by gaslight, run through my ward, and throw up the window. Poke up the fire, add blankets, joke, coax, and command; but continue to open doors and windows for a more perfect pestilence-box than this house I never saw: cold, damp, dirty, full of vile odors from wounds, kitchens, washrooms, and stables. I go to breakfast, find fried beef, salt butter, husky bread, and washy coffee.

Till noon I trot, trot, giving out rations, cutting up food for helpless "boys," washing faces, teaching my attendants how beds are made or floors are swept, dressing wounds, dusting tables, sewing bandages, keeping my tray tidy, rushing up and down after pillows, bed-linens, sponges, books, and directions. At twelve, the big bell rings and up comes dinner for the boys. When dinner is over, some sleep, many read, and others want letters written. The answering of letters after someone has died is the saddest and hardest duty a nurse has to do.

Supper at five sets everyone to running that can run; and when the flurry is over, all settle down for the evening amusements, which consist of newspapers, gossip, the doctor's last round, and, for such as need them, the final doses for the night. At nine the bell rings, gas is turned down, and day nurses go to bed. Night nurses go on duty, and sleep and death have the house to themselves.

A THIRTEEN-YEAR-OLD MAID

Anne Thackeray, Lady Ritchie (1837–1919), describes this unnamed thirteen-year-old maid of all work as "a neat, bright, clever, stumpy little thing, with a sweet sort of merrie voice," in "Maids of All Work and Blue Books", Cornhill Magazine, Septembver 1874.

Oh, I've been a servant for years! I learnt ironing off the lady; I didn't know nothing about it. I didn't know nothing about anything. I didn't know where to buy the wood for the fire; I run along the street and asked the first person I sor where the woodshop was. I was frightened—oh, I was.

They wasn't particular kind in my first place. I had plenty to eat—it wasn't anything of that. They jest give me an egg, and they says, "There, get your dinner," but not anything more. I had to do all the work. I'd no one to go to: oh! I cried the first night. I used to cry so. I had always slep in a ward full of other girls, and there I was all alone, and this was a great big house—oh, so big! and they told me to go downstairs, in a room by the kitchen all alone, with a long black passage. I might have screamed, but nobody would have heard. An archytec, the gen'l'man was. I got to break everything, oh, I was frightened!

Then I got a place in a family where there was nine children. I was about fourteen then. I earned two shillings a week. I used to get up and light the fire, bathe them and dress them, and git their breakfasts, and the lady sometimes would go up to London on business, and then I had the baby, too, and it couldn't be left, and had to be fed. I'd take them all out for a walk on the common. There was one, a cripple. She couldn't walk about.

Then there was dinner, and to wash up after; and then by that time it would be tea-time again. And then I had to put the nine children to bed and bathe them, and clean up the rooms and fires at night; there was no time in the morning. And then there would be the gen'l'man's supper to get.

Oh! that was a hard place. I wasn't in bed till twelve, and I'd be up by six. I stopped there nine months. I hadn't no one to help me. Oh yes, I had, the baker; he told me of another place. I've been there three year. I'm cook, and they are very kind, but I tell the girls there's none of 'em had such work as me. I'm very fond of reading, but I ain't no time for reading.

CLEMINTINA BLACK

Clemintina Black (1854–1922), suffragist and early trade unionist, believes domestic service is the worst work a woman can do.

That most young women of the working class dislike domestic service is generally admitted; and there is a certain inclination on the part of persons who find this dislike inconvenient to preach against it as a sort of depravity. The truth, however, is that these young women—like other classes of working people—understand their own needs and their own discomforts a great better than these are understood by their middle-class critics.

The conditions of domestic service are still those of an earlier industrial and social system, and this earlier form does not harmonize with the sentiments of today. In other employments, the person employed sells a certain number of hours of labor, and, when those hours are over, all relation ceases between employee and employer. The worker has, in short, a life of her own, absolutely apart from her industrial life.

The servant has no such life of her own. She is at beck and call from morning till night: her companions and her immediate supervisor are not of her own choosing and are not sympathetic. She is exiled from her family and from her personal friends. Smiles and civility are expected from her, whatever her mood or state of health, and whatever the conduct towards her of the persons with whom she is brought into contact, even when one of these is a son of the household in a state of intoxication.

The domestic servant, in short, still lives under a system of total personal subservience. Now, a feeling has gradually grown up that total personal subservience is intolerable and degrading, and it is this feeling which causes domestic service to be held in low social esteem by women who are often harder worked and less materially prosperous than most servants.

The servant is despised, not because she cooks, or scrubs, or nurses a baby, still less because she has to yield obedience to orders—every factory worker has to do that in working hours—but because she consents to put herself permanently at some other person's beck and call.

CATHERINE EARNSHAW

The heroine in Wuthering Heights, *Catherine Earnshaw Linton, taunts her lover, Heathcliff, who has come to see her (against her husband's wishes) in this famous scene. The lovers have been separated; Catherine has married someone else and is now dying.*

What now? You and Edgar have broken my heart, Heathcliff! And you both come to bewail the deed to me, as if you were the people to be pitied! I shall not pity you, not I. You have killed me—and thriven on it, I think. How strong you are! How many years do you mean to live after I am gone? I wish I could hold you until we were both dead! I shouldn't care what you suffered. I care nothing for your sufferings. Why shouldn't you suffer? I do! Will you forget me? Will you be happy when I am in the earth? Will you say twenty years hence, "That's the grave of Catherine Earnshaw. I loved her long ago, and was wretched to lose her; but it is past. I've loved many others since: my children are dearer to me than she was; and, at death, I shall not rejoice that I am going to her: I shall be sorry that I must leave them!" Will you say so, Heathcliff?

I'm not wishing you greater torment than I have, Heathcliff. I only wish us never to be parted: and should a word of mine distress you hereafter, think I feel the same distress underground, and for my own sake, forgive me! Come here and kneel down again! You never harmed me in your life. Nay, if you nurse anger, that will be worse to remember than my harsh words! Won't you come here again? Do!

Oh, you see, he would not relent a moment to keep me out of the grave. *That* is how I am loved! Well, never mind. That is not *my* Heathcliff. I shall love mine yet; and take him with me: he's in my soul. And the thing that irks me most is this shattered prison, after all: I'm tired, tired of being enclosed here. I'm wearying to escape into that glorious world, and to be always there: not seeing it dimly through tears, and yearning for it through the walls of an aching heart; but really with it, and in it. You think you are better and more fortunate than I; in full health and strength: you are sorry for me— very soon that will be altered. I shall be sorry for *you*. I shall be incomparably beyond and above you all.

SOPHIE

Sophie, the elderly maid in Kate Chopin's story Lilacs, *despairs at her mistress's sudden departures, which she is forced to explain. In this impassioned speech, she complains to her neighbor of her mistress's whimsical disappearances, her grizzled head quivering with emotion.*

You know, I begin to believe it is an attack of lunacy which seizes her once a year. I wouldn't say it to everyone, but with you I know it will go no further. She ought to be treated for it; a physician should be consulted; it is not well to neglect such things and let them run on.

It came this morning like a thunder clap. As I am sitting here, there had been no thought or mention of a journey. The baker had come into the kitchen—you know what a gallant he is—with always a girl in his eye. He laid the bread down upon the table and beside it a bunch of lilacs. I didn't know they had bloomed yet. "For Mam'selle Florine, with my regards," he said with his foolish simper.

Now, you know I was not going to call Florine from her work in order to present her the baker's flowers. All the same, it would not do to let them wither. I went with them in my hand into the dining room to get a majolica pitcher which I had put away in the closet there, on an upper shelf, because the handle was broken. Mademoiselle, who rises early, had just come from her bath and was crossing the hall that opens into the dining room. Just as she was, in her white *peignoir*, she thrust her head into the dining room, snuffling the air, and exclaiming, "What do I smell?"

She espied the flowers in my hand and pounced upon them like a cat upon a mouse. She held them up to her, burying her face in them for the longest time, only uttering a long "Ah!"

"Sophie, I am going away. Get out the little black trunk; a few of the plainest garments I have; my brown dress that I have not yet worn."

"But, Mademoiselle," I protested, "you forget that you have ordered a breakfast of a hundred francs for tomorrow."

"Shut up!" she cried, stamping her foot.

"You forget how the manager will rave," I persisted, "and vilify me. And you will go like that without a word of adieu to Monsieur Paul, who is an angel if ever one trod the Earth."

I tell you, Rosalie, her eyes flamed.

"Do as I tell you this instant," she exclaimed, "or I will strangle you—with your Monsieur Paul and your manager and your hundred francs!" I could well see it was insanity, and I uttered not another word as I feared for my life. I simply obeyed her every command in silence. And now—whiff, she is gone! God knows where. But between us—I wouldn't say it to Florine—but I believe it is for no good. I, in Monsieur Paul's place, should have her watched. I would put a detective upon her track.

Now I am going to close up, barricade the entire establishment. Monsieur Paul, the manager, visitors, all—all may ring and knock and shout themselves hoarse. I am tired of it all. To be vilified and called a liar—at my age!

OLIVE SCHREINER

In 1911 in Woman and War, *Olive Schreiner says women have, by their nature, a different attitude toward war than men do.*

Men's bodies are our woman's works of art. Give to us power of control—we will never carelessly throw them in to fill up the gaps in human relationships made by international ambitions and greeds. The thought would never come to us as woman, "Cast in men's bodies; settle the thing so!" Arbitration and compensation would as naturally occur to us as cheaper and simper methods of bridging the gaps in national relationships, as to the sculptor it would occur to throw in anything rather than statuary, though he might be driven to that at last!

This is one of those phases of human life, not very numerous, but very important, towards which the man as man, and the woman as woman, on the mere ground of their different sexual function with regard to reproduction, stand, and must stand, at a somewhat differing angle. The physical creation of human life, which, in as far as the male is concerned, consists in a few moments of physical pleasure, to the female must always signify months of pressure and physical endurance, crowned with danger to life. To the male, the giving of life is a laugh; to the female, blood, anguish, and sometimes death. Here we touch one of the few yet important differences between man and woman as such.

The twenty thousand men prematurely slain on a field of battle mean, to the women of their race, twenty thousand human creatures to be borne within them for months, given birth to in anguish, fed from their breast and reared with toil, if the numbers of the tribe and the strength of the nation are to be maintained. In nations continually at war, incessant and unbroken childbearing is by war imposed on all women if the state is to survive; and whenever war occurs, if numbers are to be maintained, there must be an increased childbearing and rearing. This throws upon woman as woman a war tax, compared with which all that the male expends in military preparations is comparatively light.

The relations of the female towards the production of human life influences undoubtedly even her relation towards animals and all life. "It is a fine day, let us go out and kill something!" cries the typical male of certain races, instinctively. "There is a living thing, it will die if it is not cared for," says the average woman, almost equally instinctively. It is true that the woman will sacrifice as mercilessly, as cruelly, the life of a hated rival or an enemy, as any male, *but she always knows what she is doing, and the value of the life she takes!* There is no light-hearted, careless enjoyment in the sacrifice of life to the normal woman; her instinct, instructed by practical experience, steps in to prevent it. She always knows what life costs, and that it is more easy to destroy than create it.

ELIZABETH DAY

Elizabeth Day, aged seventeen, reported what it was like to work in the mines in a report that was issued in 1842 and resulted in legislation that prohibited women and children from working in underground mines.

I have been nearly nine years in the pit. I trapped [operated doors for the trains] for two years when I first went and have hurried ever since. We always hurry in trousers as you saw us today when you were in the pit. Generally I work naked to the waist like the rest; I had my shift on today when I saw you, because I had had to wait and was cold, but generally the girls hurry naked to the waist. It is very hard work for us all. It is harder work than we ought to do a deal. I have been lamed in my ankle and strained in my back; it caused a great bone to rise in my anklebone once. The men behave well to us and never insult or ill-use us; I am sure of that. We go to work between five and six, but we begin to hurry when we get down. We stop an hour to dinner at twelve; we generally have bread and a bit of fat for dinner, and some of them a sup of beer—that's all. We have a whole hour for dinner, and we get out from to five in the evening, so that it will be eleven hours before we get out. We drink the water that runs through the pit. I am not paid wages myself; the man who employs me pays my father, but I don't know how much it is. I have never been at school. I had to begin working when I ought to have been at school. I don't go to Sunday school. The truth is, we are confined bad enough on weekdays and want to walk about on Sundays, but I go to chapel on Sunday night. I can't read at all. Jesus Christ was Adam's son, and they nailed him onto a tree, but I don't rightly understand these things.

BESSY HIGGINS

Elizabeth Gaskell's North and South *depicts the millworkers of the nineteenth century struggling to live amid terrible conditions. Bessy Higgins, sick and desperate, worries about her father, who's on strike. She's just told him his pipe smoke bothers her, and he's gone outside to finish his pipe. Now she's worried he'll be tempted to go to the local tavern to drink.*

Now am not I a fool—am I not, miss?

There, I knew I ought for to keep father at home, and away fro' the folk that are always ready for to tempt a man, in time o' strike, to go drink—and there my tongue must needs quarrel with this pipe o' his'n—and he'll go off, I know he will—as often as he wants to smoke—and nobody knows where it'll end. I wish I'd letten myself be choked first.

But what win ye have? There are days wi' you as wi' other folk, I suppose, when yo' get up and go through th' hours, just longing for a bit of a change—a bit of a fillip, as it were. I know I ha' gone and bought a four-pounder out o' another baker's shop to common on such days, just because I sickened at the thought of going on for ever wi' the same sight in my eyes, and the same thought (or no thought, for that matter) in my head, day after day, forever. I've longed for to be a man to go spreeing, even if it were only a tramp to some new place in search o' work.

And father—all men—have it stronger in 'em than me to get tired o' sameness and work forever. And what is 'em to do? It's little blame to them if they do go into th' ginshop for to make their blood flow quicker, and more lively, and see things they never see at no other time—pictures, and looking-glass, and such like. But father never was a drunkard, though maybe he's got worse for drink now and then.

Only, yo' see, at times o' strike, there's much to knock a man down, for all they start so hopefully; and where's the comfort to come fro'? He'll get angry and mad—they all do—and then get tired out wi' being angry and mad, and maybe ha' done things in their passion they'd be glad to forget. Bless yo'r sweet pitiful face! But yo' dunnot know what a strike is yet.

MARGARET FULLER

Margaret Fuller in Woman in the Nineteenth Century *defends the old maid.*

In this regard of self-dependence, and a greater simplicity and fullness of being, we must hail as a preliminary the increase of the class contemptuously designated as "old maids."

We cannot wonder at the aversion with which old bachelors and old maids have been regarded. Marriage is the natural means of forming a sphere, of taking root in the earth; it requires more strength to do this without such an opening; very many have failed, and their imperfections have been in everyone's way. They have been more partial, more harsh, more officious and impertinent, than those compelled by severer friction to render themselves endurable. Those who have a more full experience of the instincts have a distrust as to whether the unmarried can be thoroughly human and humane, such as is hinted in the saying, "Old maids' and bachelors' children are well cared for," which derides at once their ignorance and their presumption.

Yet they also gain a wider, if not so deep, experience. Those who are not intimately and permanently linked with others are thrown upon themselves; and, if they do not there find peace and incessant life, there is none to flatter them that they are not very poor and very mean.

A position which so constantly admonishes may be of inestimable benefit. The person may gain, undistracted by other relationships, a closer communion with the one. Such a use is made of it by saints and sibyls. Or she may be one of the lay sisters of charity, a canoness, bound by an inward vow—or the useful drudge of all men, the Martha, much sought, little prized—or the intellectual interpreter of the varied life she sees; the Urania of a half-formed world's twilight.

Or she may combine all these. Not "needing to care that she may please a husband," a frail and limited being, her thoughts may turn to the center, and she may, by steadfast contemplation entering into the secret of truth and love, use it for the good of all men, instead of a chosen few, and interpret through it all the forms of life. It is possible, perhaps, to be at once a priestly servant and a loving muse.

Saints and geniuses have often chosen a lonely position, in the faith that if, undisturbed by the pressure of near ties, they would give themselves up to the inspiring spirit, it would enable them to understand and reproduce life better than actual experience could.

How many "old maids" take this high stand we cannot say: it is an unhappy fact that too many who have come before the eye are gossips rather, and not always good-natured gossips. But if these abuse, and none make the best of their vocation, yet it has not failed to produce some good results. It has been seen by others, if not by themselves, that beings, likely to be alone, need to be fortified and furnished within themselves; and education and thought have tended more and more to regard these beings as related to the absolute Being, as well as to others.

It has been seen that, as the breaking of no bond ought to destroy a man, so ought the missing of none to hinder him from growing. And thus a circumstance of the time, which springs rather from its luxury than its purity, has helped to place women on the true platform.

Perhaps the next generation, looking deeper into this matter, will find that contempt is put upon old maids, or old women, at all, merely because they do not use the elixir which would keep them always young. Under its influence, a gem brightens yearly which is only seen to more advantage through the fissures Time makes in the casket.

No one thinks of Michelangelo's Persican Sibyl, or St. Theresa, or Tasso's Leonara, or the Greek Electra, as an old maid, any more than of Michelangelo or Canova as old bachelors, though all had reached the period in life's course appointed to take that degree.

GEORGE ELIOT

George Eliot (Mary Ann Evans, 1819–1880) wrote under a man's pen name, lived with a married man for twenty years, and, in general, rebelled against the nineteenth-century restrictions that bound most women. In the following description of how she began to write fiction, Eliot describes the help and support she received from George Lewes, her lifetime companion.

September 1857 made a new era in my life, for it was then I began to write fiction. It had always been a vague dream of mine that sometime or other I might write a novel, and my shadowy conception of what the novel was to be, varied, of course, from one epoch of my life to another. But I never went farther towards the actual writing of the novel than an introductory chapter describing a Staffordshire village and the life of the neighboring farm houses, and as the years passed on, I lost any hope that I should ever be able to write a novel, just as I desponded about everything else in my future.

I always thought I was deficient in dramatic power, both of construction and dialogue, but I felt I should be at my ease in the descriptive parts of a novel. My "introductory chapter" was pure description, though there were good materials in it for dramatic presentation. It happened to be among the papers I had with me in Germany, and one evening in Berlin, something led me to read it to George. He was struck with it as a bit of concrete description, and it suggested to him the possibility of my being able to write a novel, though he distrusted—indeed disbelieved in—my possession of any dramatic power. Still, he began to think that I might as well try, some time, what I could do in fiction, and by and by, when we came back to England and I had greater success than he had ever expected in other kinds of writing, his impression that it was worthwhile to see how far my mental power would go towards the production of a novel was strengthened.

He began to say very positively, "You must try and write a story," and when we were at Tenby, he urged me to begin at once. I deferred it, however, after my usual fashion, with work that does not present itself as an absolute duty. But one morning as I was lying in bed, thinking what should be the subject of my first story, my thoughts merged themselves into a dreamy doze, and I imagined myself writing a story of which the title was "The Sad Fortunes of the Reverend Amos Barton." I was soon wide awake again, and told G. He said, "O what a capital title!" and from that time I had settled in my mind that this should be my first story. George used to say, "It may be a failure—it may be that you are unable to write a fiction. Or perhaps, it may be just good enough to warrant your trying again." Again, "You may write a chef-d' oeuvre at once—there's no telling." But his prevalent impression was that, though I could hardly write a *poor* novel, my effort would want the highest quality of fiction—dramatic presentation. He used to say, "You have wit, description, and philosophy—those go a good way towards the production of a novel. It is worthwhile for you to try the experiment."

We determined that if my story turned out good enough, we would send it to Blackwood, but G. thought the more probable result was that I should have to lay it aside and try again.

But when we returned Richmond, I had to write my article on Silly Novels ["Silly Novels by Lady Novelists," *Westminster Review*] and my review of contemporary literature, so that I did not begin my story till September 22. After I had begun it, as we were walking in the park, I mentioned I had thought of a plan of writing a series of stories containing sketches drawn from clerical life opening with "Amos Barton." He at once accepted the notion as a good one—fresh and striking; and about a week afterwards when I read him the early part of "Amos," he had no longer any doubt about my ability to carry out the plan. The scene at Cross Farm, he said, satisfied him that I had the very element he had been doubtful about—it was clear I could command any pathos, and that was to be decided by the mode in which I treated Milly's death. One night G. went to town on purpose to leave me a quiet evening for writing it. I wrote the chapter from the news brought by the shepherd to Mrs. Hackit, to the moment when Amos is dragged from the bedside, and I read it to G. when he came home. We both cried over it, and then he came up to me and kissed me, saying, "I think your pathos is better than your fun."

So when the story was finished, G. sent it to Blackwood, who wrote in reply that he thought the "clerical reminiscences would do," congratulated the author of being "worthy the honors of print and pay," but would like to see more of the series before he undertook to print. However, when G. wrote that the author was discouraged by this editorial caution, Blackwood disclaimed any distrust and agreed to print the story at once. The first appeared in the January number 1857. . . . When the story was concluded, he wrote me word how Albert Smith had sent him a letter saying he had never read anything that affected him more than Milly's death, and, added Blackwood, "The men at the club seem to have mingled their tears and their tumblers together. It will be curious if you should be a member and be hearing your own praises!" There was clearly no suspicion that I was a woman. It is interesting, as an indication of the value there is in such conjectural criticism generally, to remember that when G. read the first part of "Amos" to a party . . . they were all sure I was a clergyman—a Cambridge man.

MARGARET MITCHELL WOMER

The life of women on the frontier was often hard, and little work was thought to be "unfeminine" when all hands were needed—as this memoir of Margaret Mitchell Womer, a pioneer woman in Kansas in the 1800s, details. Margaret and her five sisters did everything, including hunting and trapping.

There were nine children in our family, six girls and three boys, and as the girls were older and my father not strong, the hard toil of the pioneer life fell to the lot of the girls. We used to set traps on the banks of the Republican and catch wolves, badgers, bobcats, and skunks. Wild turkeys were very plentiful then, and we sometimes used traps to catch them.

We had some very interesting and thrilling experiences with some of the animals we caught. One day an older sister and I were out looking at our traps and noticed that a big bobcat that was caught had climbed a tree with the chain hanging to him. I sat and watched him while my sister went for a gun and shot him. Another time we killed a mother wolf and later caught her four little cubs that had fallen into a shallow well while trying to find her. One of my sisters was coming from an errand across the river when she saw five big wolves chasing a wounded buffalo. They sat on one side of the path and watched her pass, but made no effort to harm her. We saw many large herds of buffalo as they came to the river to drink, and occasionally were able to shoot one.

Our house was made of logs, and the girls helped with the construction of it. The cave we made ourselves, and were justly proud of the work, for no one in our neighborhood had a better one.

We made vinegar out of lemon juice and tapped boxelder trees for sap to make syrup, and it really was very good. We also kept a supply of skunk grease on hand in case of croup among the younger children. There were lots of fish in the river, and my sister and I became quite expert in catching them.

Sometimes there were unpleasant things to be done, but we never thought of shirking them. We had a collie dog that was a great favorite of all the family, but as her family increased too rapidly, it was decided that she must be done away with. How to kill her was a grave problem with us girls. We took her to a bluff on the river, tied one end of a rope around her neck, and fastened the other end to a tree. Then we pushed her off and ran for home. The horror of the thing is still in my mind.

ANGELA HEYWOOD

In 1893 in The Word, *Angela Heywood speaks out strongly on women's right to abortion.*

What have I thought, said, or done that anyone need be troubled about me? I come, in word expression, to establish man as man, not to demolish him. I am not proclaiming him a monster; I freight him not as disease—leave that to the "suffering sisters." Not I, but Congress-*men* force the sex issue. Is it "proper," "polite," for men, real *he*-men, to go to Washington to say, by penal law, fines, and imprisonment, whether woman may continue her natural right to wash, rinse, or wipe out her own vaginal body opening—as well as legislate when she may blow her nose, dry her eyes, or nurse her babe? Cold water prevents conception; will men therefore indict pumps and reservoirs? Whatever she may have been pleased to receive from man's own is his gift and her property. Women do not like rape and have a right to resist its results. To cut a child up in woman, procure abortion, is a most fearful, tragic deed, but *even that* does not call for man's arbitrary jurisdiction over woman's womb. I read that—

"The increase in cases of sensual criminality, affecting present morality and future generations, suggests the consideration of a remedy that may be regarded as a kindness and mercy to the offender, who seems beyond the control of his carnal passions and, being administered with the wisdom of the highest medical skill and care, would doubtless be a protection to society and productive of beneficial results. . . ."

This indicates that man is not so alarmed about preventing conception, for doth not *castration* accomplish it with a vengeance? In this proposal, do not Peace Quakers rebuke the heistic statute? Are grand jurors indeed meditating how to end the "pure" breed of

Comstocks and Parkhursts? Mrs. Caroline B. Winslow, the late Chief Justice Waite's family doctor in Washington, said as Editor of *Alpha*, to a beautiful, young wife inquiring what she should do to prevent her having *many* children, her husband being of a warm, voluptuous nature, unable to retain his life element at her touch: Mrs. Winslow said, "After all in all, Maria, I scare know what to say to thee unless thee shall use the valvet sponge."

Yes, the Comstock syringe without the gutta-percha. Then what is all this Congressional ado about? The shorter path is for man to keep his "private parts" and semen property to himself, unless he can wisely invest it in future generations. Medieval hes locked up their attractive wives' sex power and left the key with priests; their successors, legislating obscenists, commit the business to Cook, Comstock, and Parkhurst, but Gardner gets way with the key. Thus we find this aggressive cancer-plant on the body-politic and woman's body-self.

Superior to the immature animalism of Sir Phillip Sidney, Shakespeare, and Byron, Whitman portrays man's creative power worthily in "A Woman Waits For Me"; verily we exclaim with Jewish fervor, Jehovah! But in addressing "The Common Prostitute," Whitman falls to the level of David, Solomon, and Robert Browning. If woman is ever a "prostitute," who makes her such? Whitman belittles himself in expressing sympathy to a so-called fallen woman who really stands healthier than himself in the situation. She may be a "wreck" for having too trustingly served man, but does that entitle him to call her "prostitute"? I am obliged to feel that Whitman has irresponsible Solomon slyness in him, for he could not thus write to "My Girl" if he really sensed *how* she became "bad." Is he, indeed, a "libertine," ready to "enjoy" her and skulk the costs thereof? Does he cure her of "prostitution," or does he leave her more of one? Was his "significant look" a *sly wink* after all? "My Girl" *has* poetry in her, but Whitman fails to hymn it. Prostitution is not so rare an attribute as to need furtherance in songs of poets. My revolt is that Whitman holds the girl before him deprecated. Man hath no need to deal with woman's vagina, her breasts, or lips, if by so doing, in his own mind, she is hurt or defamed. Rather let him roll over on mother earth like a frenzied stallion and cry for mercy and cure.

The ground fact of woman's existence is her personality; knowledge left on me, with me, as me it is my right and duty to use. If, under sway of restrictive statutes, woman must stand still and quiver for want of wisdom to speak, allow her at least the sanctity of silence in whatever service she feels to render. Why this walk and talk in faith and practice if it is not both task and privilege for man and woman to find out what they are on this brown earth for? Law keeps up the old reign, the old disaster of hate; a new sign and saying I give unto you that ye love one another, have the joy, beauty, and plenty resulting. If Man so lot to himself and woman so as to involve *violence* in these sacred nearings, *he should have solemn meeting with and look seriously at his own penis until he is able to be lord and master of it, rather than it should longer rule, lord and master, of him and of the victims he deflowers.* Is it not he who flows semen the criminal, rather than she who disposes of it? When man learns to cease *criminating* mothers, wives, daughters, in his rude "laws," puts thoughtful injunction on himself, stops his arrogant violation of woman, we can respect him as brother, sire, mate, loving him as man, not as animal merely. St. Paul was kind enough to say that man is the head of woman; but this obscenist folly requires us to furnish brain for his —, put a *head* on man. Sex is not an unheard of or an unfelt fact in anyone, and the sooner body housekeeping has rational mention, the better. Intelligent acquaintance with and clear knowledge of ourselves will replace the song of disease with the song of health, and make home-thrift the rule, instead of the exception.

A DECLARATION

"The Women's Declaration of Sentiments" has too many uncomfortably familiar complaints, considering it was written in 1848, at the first womens' rights convention in Seneca Falls, New York.

When, in the course of human events, it becomes necessary for one portion of the family of man to assume among the people of the Earth a position different from that which they have hitherto occupied, but one to which the laws of nature and nature's God entitle them, a decent respect to the opinions of mankind requires that they should declare the causes that impel them to such a course.

We hold these truths to be self-evident: that all men women are created equal; that they are endowed by their Creator with certain inalienable rights; that among these are life, liberty, and the pursuit of happiness; that to secure these rights governments are instituted, deriving their just powers from the consent of the governed. Whenever any form of government becomes destructive of these ends, it is the right of those who suffer from it to refuse allegiance to it, and to insist upon the institution of a new government, laying its foundation on such principles, and organizing its powers in such form, as to them shall seem most likely to effect their safety and happiness. Prudence, indeed, will dictate that governments long established should not be changed for light and transient causes; and accordingly all experience hath shown that mankind are more disposed to suffer, while evils are sufferable, than to right themselves by abolishing the forms to which they are accustomed. But when a long train of abuses and usurpations, pursuing invariably the same object, evinces a design to reduce them under absolute despotism, it is their duty to throw off such government, and to provide new guards for their future security. Such has been the patient sufferance of the women under this government, and such is now the necessity which constrains them to demand the equal station to which they are entitled.

The history of mankind is a history of repeated injuries and usurpations on the part of man toward woman, having in direct object the establishment of an absolute tyranny over her. To prove this, let facts be submitted to a candid world.

He has never permitted her to exercise her inalienable right to the elective franchise.

He has compelled her to submit to laws, in the formation of which she had no voice.

He has withheld from her rights which are given to the most ignorant and degraded men—both natives and foreigners.

Having deprived her of this first right of a citizen, the elective franchise, thereby leaving her without representation in the halls of legislation, he has oppressed her on all sides.

He has made her, if married, in the eye of the law, civilly dead.

He has taken from her right in property, even to the wages she earns.

He has made her, morally, an irresponsible being, as she can commit many crimes with impunity, provided they be done in the presence of her husband. In the covenant of marriage, she is compelled to promise obedience to her husband, he becoming, to all intents and purposes, her master—the law giving him the power to deprive her of her liberty, and to administer chastisement.

He has so framed the laws of divorce, as to what shall be the proper causes, and in case of separation, to whom the guardianship of the children shall be given, as to be wholly regardless of the happiness of women—the law, in all cases, going upon a false supposition of the supremacy of man, and giving all power into his hands.

After depriving her of all rights as a married woman, if single, and the owner of property, he has taxed her to support a government which recognizes her only when her property can be made profitable to it.

He has monopolized nearly all the profitable employments, and from those she is permitted to follow, she receives but a scanty remuneration. He closes against her all the avenues to wealth and distinction which he considers most honorable to himself. As a teacher of theology, medicine, or law, she is not known.

He has denied her the facilities for obtaining a thorough education, all colleges being closed against her.

He allows her in Church, as well as State; but a subordinate position, claiming Apostolic authority for her exclusion from the ministry, and, with some exceptions, from any public participation in the affairs of the Church.

He has created a false public sentiment by giving to the world a different code of morals for men and women, by which moral delinquencies which exclude women from society, are not only tolerated, but deemed of little account in man.

He has usurped the prerogative of Jehovah himself, claiming it as his right to assign for her a sphere of action, when that belongs to her conscience and to her God.

He has endeavored, in every way that he could, to destroy her confidence in her own powers, to lessen her self-respect, and to make her willing to lead a dependent and abject life.

Now, in view of this entire disfranchisement of one-half the people of this country, their social and religious degradation—in view of the unjust laws above mentioned, and because women do feel themselves aggrieved, oppressed, and fraudulently deprived of their most sacred rights, we insist that they have immediate admission to all the rights and privileges which belong to them as citizens of the United States.

In entering upon the great work before us, we anticipate no small amount of misconception, misrepresentation, and ridicule; but we shall use every instrumentality within our power to effect our object. We shall employ agents, circulate tracts, petition the State and National legislatures, and endeavor to enlist the pulpit and the press in our behalf. We hope this Convention will be followed by a series of Conventions embracing every part of the country.

SUSAN B. ANTHONY

Before her trail for illegally voting in the 1872 election, Susan B. Anthony gave this speech.

I stand before you under indictment for the alleged crime of having voted at the last presidential election, without having a lawful right to vote. It shall be my work this evening to prove to you that in thus doing, I not only committed no crime, but instead simply exercised my citizen's rights, guaranteed to me and all United States citizens by the National Constitution, which says:

We, the people of the United States, in order to form a more perfect union, establish justice, insure domestic tranquillity, provide for the common defense, promote the general welfare, and secure the blessings of liberty to our selves and our posterity, do ordain and establish this Constitution for the United States of America.

It was we, the people, not we, the white male citizens, nor we, the male citizens; but we, the whole people, who formed this Union. We formed it not to give the blessings of liberty but to secure them; not to the half of ourselves and the half of our posterity, but to the whole people—women as well as men. It is downright mockery to talk to women of their enjoyment of the blessings of liberty while they are denied the only means of securing them provided by this democratic-republican government—the ballot.

ORDER DIRECT

MONOLOGUES THEY HAVEN'T HEARD, Karshner. Modern speeches written in the language of today. $7.95.

MORE MONOLOGUES THEY HAVEN'T HEARD, Karshner. More exciting living-language speeches. $8.95.

SCENES THEY HAVEN'T SEEN, Karshner. Modern scenes for men and women. $7.95.

FOR WOMEN: MONOLOGUES THEY HAVEN'T HEARD, Pomerance. Contemporary speeches for actresses. $7.95

MONOLOGUES for KIDS, Roddy. 28 wonderful speeches for boys and girls. $7.95.

MORE MONOLOGUES for KIDS, Roddy. More great speeches for boys and girls. $8.95.

SCENES for KIDS, Roddy. 30 scenes for girls and boys. $7.95.

MONOLOGUES for TEENAGERS, Karshner. Contemporary teen speeches. $7.95.

SCENES for TEENAGERS, Karshner. Scenes for today's teen boys and girls. $7.95.

HIGH-SCHOOL MONOLOGUES THEY HAVEN'T HEARD, Karshner. Contemporary speeches for high schoolers, $7.95.

DOWN-HOME, Karshner. Great character speeches for men and women in the language of rural America. $7.95.

MONOLOGUES from the CLASSICS, ed. Karshner. Speeches from Shakespeare, Marlowe, and others. An excellent collection for men and women, $7.95.

SCENES from the CLASSICS, ed. Maag. Scenes from Shakespeare and others. $7.95.

SHAKESPEARE'S MONOLOGUES THEY HAVEN'T HEARD, ed. Dotterer. Lesser-known speeches from The Bard. $7.95.

MONOLOGUES from CHEKHOV, trans. Cartwright. Modern translations from Chekhov's major plays: *Cherry Orchard, Uncle Vanya, Three Sisters, The Sea Gull.* $7.95.

MONOLOGUES from GEORGE BERNARD SHAW, ed. Michaels. Great speeches for men and women from the works of G.B.S. $7.95.

MONOLOGUES from OSCAR WILDE, ed. Michaels. The best of Wilde's urbane, dramatic writing from his greatest plays. For men and women. $7.95.

WOMAN, Pomerance. Monologues for actresses. $8.95.

WORKING-CLASS MONOLOGUES, Karshner. Speeches from blue-collar occupations: waitress, cleaning lady, policewoman, truck driver, miner, etc. $7.95.

MODERN SCENES for WOMEN, Pomerance. Scenes for today's actresses. $7.95.

MONOLOGUES from MOLIERE, trans. Dotterer. A definitive collection of speeches from the French Master. The first translation into English prose. $7.95.

SHAKESPEARE'S MONOLOGUES for WOMEN, trans. Dotterer. $7.95.

DIALECT MONOLOGUES, Karshner/Stern. 13 essential dialects applied to contemporary monologues. Book and cassette tape. $19.95.

YOU SAID a MOUTHFUL, Karshner. Tongue twisters galore. Great exercises for actors, singers, public speakers. Fun for everyone. $7.95.

TEENAGE MOUTH, Karshner. Modern monologues for young men and women. $8.95.

SHAKESPEARE'S LADIES, Dotterer. A second book of Shakespeare's monologues for women. With a descriptive text on acting Shakespeare. $7.95.

BETH HENLEY: MONOLOGUES FOR WOMEN, Henley. *Crimes of the Heart*, others. $7.95.

CITY WOMEN, Smith. 20 powerful, urban monologues. Great audition pieces. $7.95.

KIDS' STUFF, Roddy. 30 great audition pieces for children. $7.95.

KNAVES, KNIGHTS, and KINGS, Dotterer. Speeches for men from Shakespeare. $8.95.

DIALECT MONOLOUES, VOL II, Karshner/Stern. 14 more important dialects. Farsi, Afrikaans, Asian Indian, etc. Book and cassette tape. $19.95.

RED LICORICE, Tippit. 31 great scene-monologues for preteens. $7.95.

MODERN MONOLOGUES for MODERN KIDS, Mauro. $7.95.

SPEECHES and SCENES from OSCAR'S BEST FILMS, Dotterer. $19.95.

A WOMAN SPEAKS: WOMEN FAMOUS, INFAMOUS and UNKNOWN, Cosentino. $12.95.

Send your check or money order (no cash or COD) plus handling charges of $4.00 for the first book and $1.50 for each additional book. California residents add 8.25 % tax. Send your order to: Dramaline Publications, 36-851 Palm View Road, Rancho Mirage, California 92270.